LIES
PASTORS
BELIEVE

T0019618

"Daily I have to remind myself that as a pastor I'm no more holy than any other saint and no less human. *Lies Pastors Believe* is a timely reminder that a pastor's identity, peace, and mission are found in Christ alone. Nothing and no one else. This book will challenge you to turn your eyes upon Jesus and walk in a necessary humility to care for his sheep."

—D. A. HORTON, pastor, Reach Fellowship (North Long Beach, CA); chief evangelist, Urban Youth Workers Institute

"Success is not defined by the size of your platform. Success is about faithfulness to God and faithfully stewarding what and who he's entrusted to you. Dayton has done a great job outlining the temptations we all face as pastors. Don't miss this important message."

—DANIEL IM, author of *No Silver Bullets*; coauthor of *Planting Missional Churches*; director of church multiplication at NewChurches.com; teaching pastor, The Fellowship (Nashville, TN)

"There's not much glamorous about being a shepherd. We all know that, and we'd all remember that if not for the lies we pastors can too easily believe. In this short book, Dayton Hartman slices through the smog of prideful ambition and brings us back to the basics of what it means to serve Jesus' church. Dayton has written honestly, which might feel painful at times, but it's helpful, and that's why this is an important resource for every minister of the gospel."

—JONATHAN PARNELL, lead pastor, Cities Church (Minneapolis, MN); author of *Never Settle for Normal*

"Dayton Hartman shows great maturity in the way he addresses some of the lies that church leaders are tempted to believe whilst wooing our hearts with the compelling beauty of Christ. Read and enjoy. I'm certain you'll be refreshed, challenged, and encouraged in your work for the Lord."

—STEVE TIMMIS, CEO, Acts 29

"Satan tells the same lies to every pastor that he told to Adam in the garden. If you wonder why some of your greatest heroes in the faith stumble and fall, this book will remind you that nobody is exempt from Adam's sin, but thank God nor do we ever graduate from his gracious solution. Indwelling sin, and the power of Satan, are real. So is God's greater grace."

—J. D. Greear, pastor, The Summit Church
(Raleigh-Durham, NC); author of *Gaining by Losing*

"I'm convinced that it is not only possible but in many cases probable that a pastor will give his life to a career rather than a calling. When this line is blurred, all sorts of deceptions arise. Dayton addresses some old sins with updated faces, unmasking them with the good news of the gospel, helpfully directing readers back to Jesus, the head of the Church."

—Alex Early, pastor of preaching and theology,
Redemption Church (Seattle, WA);
author of *The Reckless Love of God*
and *The New Believer's Guide to the Christian Life*

"I am grateful for men like Dayton who are helping pastors think deeply about the state of their soul. I have served as a pastor for nearly 20 years now and I am acutely aware of how powerful and persistent the lies can be that would threaten to derail my life and ministry. This treatment from Dayton is a necessary corrective and a helpful grace for the pastor. I hope you will give this book the attention it deserves."

—Micah Fries, senior pastor,
Brainerd Baptist Church (Chattanooga, TN)

LIES
PASTORS
BELIEVE

7 WAYS TO ELEVATE YOURSELF,
SUBVERT THE GOSPEL,
AND UNDERMINE THE CHURCH

DAYTON HARTMAN

LEXHAM PRESS

Lies Pastors Believe: 7 Ways to Elevate Yourself, Subvert the Gospel, and Undermine the Church

Copyright 2017 Dayton Hartman

Lexham Press, 1313 Commercial St., Bellingham, WA 98225
www.lexhampress.com

You may use brief quotations from this commentary in presentations, articles, and books. For all other uses, please write Lexham Press for permission. Email us at permissions@lexhampress.com.

Print ISBN 9781683590385
Digital ISBN 9781683590392

Lexham Editorial Team: Elliot Ritzema, David Bomar
Cover Design: Brittany Schrock
Back Cover Design: Liz Donovan
Typesetting: ProjectLuz.com

To my students and interns:
Love truth and reject lies.

Contents

Acknowledgments

I owe a great debt of gratitude to Brannon Ellis and Todd Hains for their belief in this book. Additionally, Elliot Ritzema's efforts toward refining the content of this book made it much better than it otherwise could have been. Moreover, I'm very grateful for Josh Wester working through my initial manuscript with me and for Erik Harris giving me his chapter-by-chapter feedback. Finally, I thank my wife for her constant encouragement to be honest regarding my own failures as a pastor.

INTRODUCTION

LIAR, LIAR

W e all believe lies. Not only do we believe lies, but we lie to ourselves constantly, endlessly.

Perhaps this affinity for lies is nowhere better demonstrated than the 1997 hit movie *Liar Liar*. I remember watching this movie at a friend's house using a filtering service that screened out morally questionable scenes and vulgar language. Of course, watching *Liar Liar* this way made it a very short movie. Still, I managed to get the gist, and aside from the (fragmented) humor what struck me the most was its stunning portrayal of the human heart's love of lies.

In the movie, a young boy makes a birthday wish that his dad, a chronic liar (played by Jim Carrey), would be forced to tell the truth. Miraculously, the wish comes true. The boy's father is forced to speak and act with total honesty at all times. What follows is a comedic montage showing the horror and pain of being forced to tell the truth—and the utter misery of being regularly confronted with the truth. While telling the truth is held up as a virtue, the film rightly observes that humans generally find life to be more comfortable when we can tell and believe lies.

Here Hollywood got it right: Only a miracle stops us from being drawn to lies. As Christians, this shouldn't surprise us. Every time we sin, we believe lies: We believe that God is not good, he does not love us, and he has not met our greatest need. Our hearts, apart from God's regenerating grace, are literally lie-producing and lie-believing machines (Jer 17:9). As sinners, you could say that lies are our native language.

It is only through the Spirit's sanctifying work that we continually grow in Christlikeness, which includes increasing love for, belief in, and communication of truth. Yet as works in progress (Phil 1:6), we are still constantly tempted to deceive ourselves and others. You lied to yourself this morning, didn't you? You ate a Krispy Kreme doughnut for breakfast, convincing yourself you will be walking a lot and burning off the calories during the day. What are you doing right now? Sitting and reading this book. Liar!

As each year of ministry passes, I'm amazed by the lies I have believed. As I've matured, I've found that one of the best defenses against believing lies is knowing the kinds of lies that tempt me. I'm on guard for them before I believe them, and so the temptation to believe and speak things I know are untrue has increasingly diminished. But still, even with greater awareness, I'm continually identifying lies that I tell myself.

I've also found that other pastors are tempted to believe many of the same lies I have accepted. As a result I have concluded that pastors have a unique subset of lies they are tempted to believe. In this book, I want to lay bare these lies. While I cannot exhaustively address every lie that any individual pastor might be drawn to, I'm convinced that pastors are uniquely tempted to believe lies related to their identity *as pastors*.

One of the greatest temptations for those in ministry is to tie our identity to what we accomplish rather than what Christ has accomplished. The danger in believing lies about our identity, even small ones, is that a seemingly inconsequential deception always gives way to a larger deception. What begins as a small lie we believe about ourselves often leads to taking our eyes off Christ and ignoring our moral failures. There is no such thing as a harmless lie.

In addition to being a pastor, I'm also a seminary professor tasked with equipping men who want to be pastors.[1] One of the constant refrains of my life in ministry has been "Why didn't anyone warn me that I would be constantly battling self-deception?" If you are a seminary student, my hope is that my openness will help you guard against specific lies. These are lies I've had to battle and lies I've seen many of my students believe, as well.

On the other hand, if you have been a pastor for a while, you are probably more aware of the lies you've told yourself than you are willing to admit. I get it. It's a humiliating thing to recognize how badly you have misled yourself. Still,

---

1. I want to be clear from the outset that I am approaching the subject of pastoral ministry as a committed complementarian, meaning in part that I believe the Bible teaches that the office of pastor/elder is to be occupied by biblically qualified males. While those who hold to egalitarianism may find this book useful, my language throughout presupposes that pastors are men. For more information on this issue, I recommend Thomas R. Schreiner and Andreas J. Kostenberger, eds., *Women in the Church: An Analysis and Application of 1 Timothy 2:9–15*, 2nd ed. (Grand Rapids: Baker Academic, 2005).

as you read each of the following chapters, be open to considering how you may have been deceived by similar lies. Ignoring the lies you've believed will not protect you, your family, or your church from the eventual fallout. Therefore, you must begin rooting out the idols of your heart that give rise to the deceptions you so willingly embrace. You cannot be passive in the war against self-deception. Be on guard!

Whether you are preparing for ministry or are serving in ministry now, consider inviting a fellow seminary student or pastor to read this book with you, ask you the reflection questions at the end of each chapter, and give you honest feedback. There is great freedom and true joy in facing the truth. However, merely identifying the lies you've believed does not resolve the problem. We must respond to our self-deception with corrective actions. That is why I have suggested a series of action steps to help you overcome the lies you've believed.

Pastors (and future pastors), the way to win the war on lies is to speak truth, believe truth, and constantly be reminded of truth.

1

THE VISIONARY

"Jesus has called me to lead a movement"

In seminary, I had a major ego problem (admittedly, I still do from time to time). I wasn't exactly the Kanye West or Justin Bieber of the Baptist classroom, but I really thought I was being prepared to do something big for the name of Jesus. I envisioned myself teaching large crowds, seeing hundreds—no, wait—*thousands* come to Christ every time I preached. It was lunacy! Not because Jesus cannot do big things, but because I can't. What I was imagining as my future was really more about me than the kingdom of Christ.

It never struck me how strange and self-aggrandizing this whole mindset was until I was sitting in class one day. Our professor asked us to apply a theological concept to local church ministry, and his question presupposed a church of about 100–300 people. A student raised his hand and gave an outlandish answer. When the professor asked him to clarify what he was saying, he said something like this: "Oh, I'm sorry. The Lord has called me to lead and

pastor a megachurch, so I was applying it to *my* calling."
The professor just stared, chuckled a little, and moved on.

In that moment, the Spirit began to cause me to see
that I and many of my fellow seminarians were viewing
the local church as a means to an end. In an age of celebrity pastors, the conference circuit, and personality-driven
ministry, many of us were ready and willing to jump into
the machine and become another "product" to be sold, mar-
keted, and embraced by the Christian masses. (For the
record, that student hasn't led a megachurch.)

As I emerged from the heady atmosphere of seminary,
I just assumed that the longer I was in ministry the more
I would see the antithesis of this attitude among the pas-
tors I would serve alongside. While I believe most pastors
are driven by a desire to humbly serve their congregations,
I am still shocked by how many think they are destined to
have the influence of men like John Piper, Tim Keller, and
R. C. Sproul.

All of us are excited by the prospect of leaving a great
legacy, of being used by God in ways that will echo long
beyond our lifetime. That's not a bad thing. The problem
is we misunderstand what it means to leave a legacy and
be used by God.

The Mighty Have Fallen

Every time a well-known or celebrity pastor[1] has to leave
the ministry, people want to know why. How could men

---

1. While some use the term "celebrity pastor" in a derogatory manner,
my intention is simply to acknowledge that some pastors are so well
known that they've reached what our culture would call "celebrity status."

of God, who seemingly have all the answers, fail? On the most obvious level, they fail because they are sinners, and sinners will sin. Nevertheless, the downfall of celebrity pastors is usually a direct result of their pursuit of a platform, their desire to begin or lead a movement, their drive to achieve big things for themselves. While all pastors are still sinners, the particular danger of this lie is that if you make your ministry about you, the fallout of your sin will be even worse than it would have been otherwise.

At the heart of this lie is the desire for significance, relevance, recognition, and influence based on our own gifts. It is, in short, pride. It is the desire for power over others to bend them to our will. We see our congregations as a means to our own end rather than as people who are highly valued by God, and for whom Christ died.

Sometimes believing this lie leads to an explicit moral failure. The evangelical church in the United States has seen too many well-known pastors leave their ministries in disgrace. Constant attempts to increase numbers (of both people and dollars), to write books, to speak at conferences, and to cast one's own vision are exhausting. Even when things are going well, there is pressure to keep expanding your platform. This pressure can drive some pastors to try to cope in unhealthy ways. One pastor may engage in adultery or inappropriate relationships. Another may not commit adultery, but his marriage still collapses under the pressure he puts on himself. Still other pastors may become addicted to alcohol or drugs. All this may come from a struggle to cope with the extraordinary pressure of casting our own vision and leading a movement.

At other times, however, there may be no hint of what we would usually call a moral failure. Instead, there is simply the quiet swelling of the ego, the shifting to a more auto-cratic style of leadership, the manipulation of other people to build our own significance. While this is less shocking and less likely to make the news, it is no less serious.

Once a pastor has left the ministry as a result of believing the lie of the achiever, there is still hope. Some pastors accept responsibility for their sin. They accept the charges that their ego was out of control and that they had relentlessly pursued the building of their platform. They acknowledge that their identity was wrapped up in their own name recognition, rather than in the name above all names. While the falls of these pastors send shockwaves, their repentance can go on to provide comfort. When pastors own their sin and express their need for prayer and forgiveness, sometimes they may be restored to a humbler and more faithful form of ministry.

Shepherds Anonymous

While there is the possibility of repentance and restoration after believing this lie, it would be better to not believe the lie in the first place. We can avoid it by paying closer attention to a biblical metaphor about pastors. The Bible talks about pastoring in terms of shepherding (Acts 20:28; 1 Pet 5:1–3), and shepherding isn't meant to be glamorous. The reason shepherding is such a perfect analogy for pastoral ministry is that it is often hard, unrecognized work for the good of those who may never thank you. The Bible mentions many shepherds, but it names only a few.

On the fateful day Joseph becomes a slave, he is walking around the fields of Shechem, looking for his brothers, when he encounters a man—presumably a shepherd. This shepherd tells Joseph, "I heard your brothers saying they were going to Dothan" (see Gen 37). If this busybody shepherd doesn't run into Joseph wandering in a pasture, Joseph is never betrayed by his brothers and sold into slavery. He never goes to Egypt and never saves the nations. Instead, everyone dies of famine and the bloodline of the Messiah is eradicated. So this shepherd is pretty important to the history of salvation, yet he is nameless! It is the same with the shepherds at the birth of Christ.

Even the few shepherds whose names we know are most important for their role in the narrative of redemption. Moses, the deliverer, was once a shepherd. Then Jesus came along—the true and better deliverer! David went from being a shepherd to being a king, and his bloodline carried the lineage of the Messiah. Then Jesus came along as the Son of David who is the King of kings. The fame of these shepherds points to Jesus, the only Shepherd who saves.

Who Is Pastor Steve?

Not enough pastors desire to be Steve Lewis.

The city where I pastor is full of people whose faith was shaped by "Pastor Steve." He was a man who truly believed the gospel, faithfully served his church, and then died. To my knowledge, Steve never wrote a book or spoke at a major conference. He didn't have a blog or his own personal logo. He was simply a faithful pastor whose gospel legacy has lived on well beyond his earthly life. He never became famous, but he did make Jesus famous.

With so many guys aiming to be the next great conference speaker, I fear few will ever become Steve Lewis. Not enough young pastors recognize that pastoral ministry isn't flashy; it is faithful service. It isn't about building a brand; it is about pointing people to Jesus. It isn't about growing a platform; it is about advancing the kingdom. In my own denomination, the Southern Baptist Convention, there are roughly 46,000 active senior pastors. The work of those shepherds whose name is never known by anyone outside their congregation is just as central to Christ's plan to build his church and save sinners as the work of pastors with major name recognition.

Now, it is not a sin to have a large influence. The sin is when a pastor allows himself to take a place that only Jesus can take. This is a real temptation, since it is not uncommon for congregations to subconsciously place sinners in a position that only the Savior can occupy. This happens in churches small and large. People associate a congregation with its pastor to such an extent that they call it "Pastor so-and-so's" church.

Faced with this reality, pastors willingly allow themselves to take the seat that belongs only to Jesus. But when we begin to believe that a church is *our* church, we've taken the place of Christ. When we allow the congregation to believe it's because of our clever and engaging sermons that sinners are being redeemed, rather than through Christ's work in the hearts of men and women, we are taking people's hopes and placing them on our shoulders. We cannot be the hope for our congregations; only Jesus can be their hope. Our job is not to cast our vision; our job is to announce Jesus's promise to save sinners and change nations. The hope we give people is not that we will lead them into an exciting future of gospel transformation, but that Jesus has already purchased the guarantee of a world transformed by the gospel.

Pastors (and future pastors) who presume that God is going to give them a large platform are seeing the church, the bride of Christ, as something to use for selfish gain rather than a people to love and serve. If you use the church for your own advantage, you've begun abusing someone else's bride. The church's Bridegroom spoke the universe into existence, died, and came back from the dead, and is returning with a mysterious name tattooed on his thigh and the power to strike down the nations with his words (Rev 19:11–16). As a general rule, don't mess with guys who have thigh tattoos. They are tougher than you.

When we willingly claim the role of hero, we will always become the villain. We can avoid the lie of a super-sized ministry by reminding ourselves that Jesus is the hero, not us. One of the ways I try to protect my heart from this lie is to constantly remind myself that God has called pastors to a ministry of death to self: Death in me, life in the church family (2 Cor 4:12). The truth is, pastors don't have all the answers; we just know the One who does. And he has two nail-pierced feet.

So do not shirk your duties or despise your office because Christ has not given you a large platform. Your calling isn't to fame; it's to the difficult task of loving and caring for the sheep Jesus has sought and purchased. Augustine of Hippo once summarized the responsibilities of a pastor this way (a quote I come back to often):

> The turbulent have to be corrected, the faint-hearted cheered up, the weary supported; the gospel's opponents need to be refuted, its insidious enemies guarded against; the unlearned need to be taught, the indolent stirred up, the argumentative checked; the proud must be put in their place, the desperate set on their feet, those engaged in quarrels reconciled; the needy have to be helped, the oppressed to

be liberated, the good to be given your backing, the
bad to be tolerated; all must be loved. (*Sermon* 340.1)
That's not glamorous, but it is our job.

Conclusion

I'm aware of the apparent irony in writing this chapter.
A guy who has written books telling guys not to write books
or speak at conferences? Well, not exactly. What I am saying
is that if you serve Christ as a faithful pastor and, in the
midst of this service, God gives you a larger platform, then
use it well. But don't aim for fame. Instead, work hard and
pray that God will keep you faithful. C. S. Lewis wrote, "You
can't get second things by putting them first; you can get
second things only by putting first things first."[2] If you aim
for fame over faithfulness, you will end up frustrated and
unfulfilled, always striving to make a name for yourself. If
you aim for faithfulness, it's possible that you may get fame
thrown in—but it won't control you. You'll be able to hold
it lightly and recognize that it's fleeting.

If you think Jesus has called you to create a brand and
market yourself as a celebrity pastor, here is what I can tell
you for sure: No, he hasn't! Jesus has called you to serve as
an under-shepherd for him as he shepherds his church.
It's not that he needs you; it's just that, in his grace, he has
given you a seat on the bench so you can be part of the team.
Do not seek great things for yourself (Jer 45:5).

If you believe the lie that Jesus has called you to lead
a movement, then the only movement you've been called

---

2. C. S. Lewis, "First and Second Things," in *God in the Dock*, ed. Walter
Hooper (New York: HarperOne, 1994), 310.

to is ushering yourself out of the pulpit and into the pew.
Stay humble, stay faithful, serve well—and be forgotten.

REFLECTION QUESTIONS

1. How often do I envision fame for my name rather than
   the increased fame of Jesus' name?

2. Do I shirk the difficult tasks of pastoral ministry because
   I feel they are beneath me?

3. How drawn am I to a ministry that will bring me notoriety versus a ministry that no one will ever know about?

4. How often do I feel like the church owes me something?

5. Am I content to love the people Christ has entrusted to me, or am I using them to gain opportunities for myself?

ACTION STEPS

1. Ask other elders or pastors in your congregation for accountability regarding your motives and your opportunities for recognition.

2. Build into your weekly routine some kind of humbling form of service to the local church, and make it a point to not seek recognition for it.

3. At regular intervals, meet with a biblical counselor or other pastors who will ask probing questions to ascertain the condition of your heart.

2

THE IRON CHEF

"No one has ever fed them like me"

One of my guilty pleasures in seminary was to binge-watch TV marathons of *Iron Chef*. No, not *Iron Chef America*. I'm talking about the original Japanese show, complete with voiceovers. The premise was simple: Two chefs, pitted against each other in a kitchen that looked like a gladiator arena, were tasked with making several dishes that featured the same primary ingredient. The difference between winning and losing, between success and failure, was entirely up to the presentation and arrangement of the ingredients. Watching someone make a three-course meal, along with a dessert, out of octopus is one of the most strangely satisfying things you could ever witness.

A few years after seminary, the lessons I learned from all those hours watching *Iron Chef* were still with me. In one of my ministry assignments, I preached a sermon that elicited far more praise than it deserved. Numerous congregants approached me and told me things like, "You are so gifted! You need to preach here more often!" Others said things like, "No one has ever fed my soul like you!" I took it all in and believed every word of it. Just like on *Iron Chef*, the presentation makes all the difference. And I thought I was good at it!

As my preaching load increased, I heard more and more compliments. My self-confidence soared, as did my ego. However, it all came crashing down because of two things I overheard. First, after a guest speaker finished his sermon, the same person who told me I fed them like no one else said those exact words to our guest preacher. I felt betrayed. I mean, his sermon wasn't *that* good. Second, I learned that one of those who acted as my biggest cheerleader had a secret agenda: to use my preaching to try and drive a wedge between me and the primary teaching pastor. The goal was nefarious and the plan was working masterfully. I was sickened.

Empty Calories

One of the saddest things I've ever seen in ministry was the life of a pastor who had successfully revitalized a church. Young and recently graduated from seminary, this man became pastor of a congregation that had dwindled from 150–200 people on a Sunday morning to no more than a couple dozen. After about a year in the pulpit, this very gifted communicator had led the church on a massive turnaround, and regular attendance grew by well over a hundred people. As a result, this pastor attracted wider attention in our community. Yet, not two years into his tenure, cracks began to form in his ministry. People were constantly telling him that he was gifted and that God had big plans for him. Many of his congregants told him that they had never heard preaching like his before and that one day he would surely be famous. And he believed every single word of it.

He then began privately boasting about how he was the best preacher for at least a few hundred miles. Perhaps he was the best expositor in North Carolina. He even went so far as to tell a group of pastors that he was on the verge of developing a huge platform for ministry that would gain him national recognition. About six months passed and nothing had happened. There was no big breakthrough, no national recognition, no conference invitations. In his frustration, he began seeking something, anything, to make him feel empowered. So, he began having an affair with what he called "the most attractive woman in the church." His rationale: If she wanted a relationship with him, then he must be special, unique, and impressive. He was looking for a functional savior.

A few months into the affair, his wife found out. Their marriage collapsed. The church imploded, and the name of Jesus was marred. Now, five years later, that church is barely limping along as it attempts to rebuild its credibility in the community. That pastor is now divorced. His ex-wife and children will forever be scarred by what started as a seemingly innocent belief: "No one has ever fed us like you."

Even if this lie doesn't lead to a moral failure, it still causes great harm. Over the past few months, I've started listening to the sermons of one of the most well-known "celebrity pastors" in the United States. This man is an unbelievably effective communicator. His command of language, his hold over an audience, and his ability to draw in listeners are almost without equal. Yet what I have found striking about this man's sermons is how empty they are.

There's almost no reading of Scripture, let alone exposition of the text. Instead, he tells his audience that God has given him a "word." It's all very practical, all very helpful, and almost totally divorced from the Scriptures, the work of Christ, and grace. Even more, there is no respect for the holiness of God.

Yet things have not always been this way. I remember listening to this man's early sermons (many years ago) and they contained all the necessary ingredients of a Christ-honoring sermon. Nevertheless, as this pastor's platform grew, he began dropping the exposition of Scripture in favor of his masterful communication abilities and creative illustrations. Now, many years later, his sermons are filled with attention-grabbing insights, but they lack the Scriptures. His messages are full of good things, but devoid of Good News. I'm convinced this is the natural progression when we assume that we ourselves, rather than Scripture, are the necessary ingredient to good preaching. If you want empty sermons, make sure you and your personality take center stage. On the other hand, if you desire to serve your people a feast of truth, ensure that your sermons are full of Scripture, God-centered theology, and gospel grace. When we become focused primarily on what *we* have to say, we end up saying nothing at all.

The Ingredient List

After the shock of finding out that people weren't complimenting my preaching out of pure motives, I paid extra-close attention to every detail of the preaching pastor's sermons. They were good! They were quite different in style from my own, but they were excellent sermons. This launched me into a months-long survey of preaching styles, as I took note of good and not-so-good sermons by well-known preachers. I listened to as much preaching as my ears could stand—John Piper, Ligon Duncan, Thabiti Anyabwile, Matt Chandler, Eric Mason, Tony Merida, J. D. Greear, Mark Dever, H. B. Charles Jr., and John MacArthur. My conclusion? They were all very good preachers, and yet they were all very *different* preachers.

What made their sermons so good is that they all used the same ingredients: Christ-centered exposition, a high view of God, and a hearty helping of scandalous gospel grace. The only difference was in how they assembled and presented the ingredients. It turns out good sermons aren't like *Iron Chef* after all. The key isn't the style or manner of presentation (although that is important); the key is the ingredient list!

Let me just say this as straightforwardly as I can:

1) You are not as good a preacher as you think you are.
2) Many of the compliments you've received are likely meant to stroke your ego, further an agenda, or to simply be polite.
3) No matter how convinced you are of your giftedness in the pulpit, you are not actually doing anything different from the many pastors who have come before you. Sure, your specific presentation of the necessary ingredients of a good sermon may be nuanced by your personality, but you are serving up the same meal as everyone else who preaches the gospel.

True, someone in your church might have told you that you preach in a way that no pastor (or at least their last pastor) ever has. But unless this person has come from a gospel-less church, they're telling you a lie. All gospel-focused, Christ-honoring, expositional-sermon-preaching pastors are serving the same meat and potatoes in their sermons. I'm all for careful preparation and striving for excellence, but the meals you're providing in your sermons are *not* better than those of any other faithful preacher. You may garnish the serving dish differently, but you didn't make the meal.

Listen Intently, Read Widely

Once you realize that your ability to communicate Scripture isn't something to be prideful over—and that you're not as good a preacher as you assume—you're faced with the following tension: "How do I continue to become a better preacher while at the same time growing in my sense of humility in the pulpit?" I don't believe there is a one-size-fits-all answer, but two things I recommend are listening intently and reading widely.

First, listen intently. Observe good expositors and take note of how they highlight Jesus or the gospel in any given text. Pay close attention to how they turn a phrase in a heart-grabbing moment of textual application. Emulate their faithfulness to the text without emulating their style. Your unique personality has been created by God and is used in your communication of his word. Be yourself in the pulpit, but be shaped by the faithful preaching of other pastors. I also strongly recommend a steady diet of sermons from pastors of varying traditions, ethnicities, and styles. Acquainted with a variety of preachers, you will be able to see how they relate the gospel to different audiences, and you will be less tempted to imitate any one of them.

Second, read widely. One of the most useful and humbling resources I have found for my own development as a preacher has been church history. No matter how well I may articulate a doctrine, Jonathan Edwards (1703–1758) did it better. That's humbling. Just when I think I've waxed eloquent, I realize I'm nothing more than a poorly contextualized, everything-must-be-said-in-140-characters-or-less echo of what Edwards said masterfully.

When I look over the manuscripts of even my best sermons, they read like poorly written knock-offs of good sermons from men like John Chrysostom (349–407). Chrysostom—whose name means literally, "John with the golden tongue"—is one of the greatest preachers in church history. I strongly encourage regular reading of his sermons and biblical commentaries. This is from one of his Easter sermons, talking about the resurrection defeating hell:

> Hell was in an uproar because it was done away with.
> It was in an uproar because it is mocked.
> It was in an uproar, for it is destroyed.
> It is in an uproar, for it is annihilated.
> It is in an uproar, for it is now made captive.
> Hell took a body, and discovered God.
> It took earth, and encountered Heaven.
> It took what it saw, and was overcome by what it
>   did not see.
> O death, where is thy sting?
> O Hades, where is thy victory?
>
> Christ is Risen, and you, O death, are annihilated!
> Christ is Risen, and the evil ones are cast down!
> Christ is Risen, and the angels rejoice!
> Christ is Risen, and life is liberated!
> Christ is Risen, and the tomb is emptied of its dead;

for Christ having risen from the dead,
is become the first-fruits of those who have
    fallen asleep.

To Him be Glory and Power forever and ever. Amen![1]

While the style is better suited to Chrysostom's fourth-century Constantinople than to modern America, this is still better than your (and my) best Easter sermon. No wonder it is read aloud every year in Eastern Orthodox churches! Even though none of us have ever preached something this good, reading great sermons from the past constantly prompts me to think through this question: "How do I preach like that in a twenty-first century context?" Reading church history will humble you and equip you to be a better pastor and a better preacher.

Write Sermons in Community

While listening intently and reading widely are good ways to begin the process of staying humble while improving your preaching, an even more effective practice for me has been our church's practice of writing sermons in community. The first time I heard Mark Dever, pastor of Capitol Hill Baptist Church, explain the value of performing a group sermon review after each Sunday's message, it seemed crazy to me. How could you ever preach a sermon in front of people who are examining every word with a critical ear? How do you preach to those who are preparing to give you verbal pushback?

---

1. John Chrysostom, "Hell Took a Body and Discovered God," http://www.christianitytoday.com/ct/2000/aprilweb-only/13.ob.html.

This reminded me of the TV show *American Idol* (which I never liked). While part of me took some sick pleasure in watching people act like they're the next Adele while sounding more like Clint Eastwood, I found the premise of having a panel of judges publically critique people to be terrifying. I thought doing a group sermon review would be like inviting my church's Simon Cowell to lambast me with harsh criticism for no good reason. Yikes! But this is the kind of thing you need to help you stop believing the lie that the main ingredient in good preaching is you.

Our church has instituted weekly reviews of each Sunday's sermon, and it has produced exactly what Dever promised it would: clarity in gospel communication. Each Thursday, our staff and interns meet to review the sermon manuscript for the message to be delivered on Sunday. Then, on the following Tuesday, we review the message that was delivered. The benefits of this practice are numerous. Let me encourage you with a few of the most important:

Sermon review increases gospel clarity. Having multiple eyes on your manuscript and multiple, critical sets of ears listening to your sermon will increase the care with which you communicate the gospel and exposit the text.

Sermon review makes your sermons better. The Spirit draws us into community and gives each of us unique, complementary gifts. Nearly every week, our sermon reviews produce some of the best content found in each week's message. The collective wisdom and insight of men who love Jesus and love your congregation will help you better apply the text to the hearts of your people.

Sermon review produces humility. It is an incredibly humbling thing to invite criticism. Preaching is already a very "exposing" exercise as you pour out your soul in front of your congregation. It leaves you feeling vulnerable. Thus, inviting critical feedback and comments seems like madness, but it isn't. It only serves to encourage your heart and to produce increased humility before your people and your leadership team. We all need more humility.

Sermon review builds good preachers. A regular review process is immensely beneficial for younger preachers on a teaching team. We've seen the incredible value of this practice in equipping our interns (future pastors and church planters) as they are invited into the sermon prep, delivery, and feedback process. If you want to build preachers, this process is a must.

This process is meant to ensure that we are doing the very thing Paul has commanded us to do: rightly handle the Scriptures (2 Tim 2:15). Jesus saved us and made us part of a people. All of the Christian life is meant to be lived in community. Why then would we assume that the central practice of the Christian rhythm of life (the proclaiming and hearing of the Scriptures) ought to be accomplished in isolation? No! The crafting of the sermon ought to take place in the same way the hearing of the sermon occurs— in community!

In short, inviting more cooks into the kitchen will produce a better meal of gospel clarity while reinforcing the awareness that you are simply presenting the same ingredients as many other faithful expositors in your church and around the world. The more we can be reminded that it's the ingredients of the sermon that matter, the more we will work to make sure the ingredients are what take center stage. When we become consumed with our ability to present the ingredients, we will abandon the ingredients in favor of our favorite garnishing techniques.

Conclusion

Those of us who are faithful to the Scriptures must preach with a Christ-centered hermeneutic, a high view of God, and a celebration of grace. What matters is that all those ingredients are present. As you work out the stylistic details of how you present the Scriptures in your preaching, keep in mind that some of the praise you've received for your ability to preach might be warranted. Some pastors are genuinely gifted communicators. However, some praise might be tied to an agenda that involves stroking your ego, a desire to be polite, personal preferences, or someone wanting to encourage you simply because they like you as a person.

It is equally true that some of the criticisms you've received are valid. However, some criticism is likely tied to your listener's personal preferences. So instead of focusing on the praise or criticism you receive, remember that you are but one in a long line of gospel communicators. You are nothing more and nothing less than an instrument of grace in the hands of the only One who truly preaches with authority: Jesus. So, garnish the meal well with your own style, but recognize that the meat and potatoes you serve are the same as what every other gospel communicator is offering. Don't get cocky. We all offer up the same Bread of Life.

REFLECTION QUESTIONS

1. When I write a sermon, is my first thought "What does the text say?" or "What can I say about this text?"

2. Do I outline a passage looking for how it points readers/hearers to Christ, or how it can point to what I want to communicate?

3. How do I respond when people compliment my sermon (not just outwardly, but inwardly)? Am I humbled by the working of the word or am I proud of my own communication abilities?

4. How willing am I to be critiqued, examined, and engaged by others over what I am or am not preaching?

5. How often do I welcome critical feedback on my sermon content or presentation?

ACTION STEPS

1. Invite your church leaders into your sermon writing and sermon review process.

2. Critically assess the motivations and goals of your heart as you think about your preaching.

3. Consume Christ-honoring sermons from throughout church history and today.

4. Seek out constructive feedback. When you are corrected, receive it in a spirit of openness and a desire to improve.

3

THE ACHIEVER

"Jesus loves me,
this I earn"

A good friend of mine had been a pastor for a number of years and his congregation adored him. He was folksy in a way that wasn't cheesy, but was truly endearing—think *Hee-Haw*, minus the Hee (and the Haw). He was kind and made time for everyone in the church. He never missed a chance to encourage older saints in the twilight years of life. Then he offended the wrong family and a firestorm of rumors began to swirl about him. Some of the charges were absurd and mean-spirited. After a few months of this "living nightmare," as he described it, he finally broke. His response to the church was angry, even vicious, almost enraged. He felt validated in attempting to deliver a heavy-handed "knockout blow" to those opposing and criticizing him.

He reached out to me, and we began to talk through all that was going on. As I attempted to probe into his soul, I found that he was a deeply wounded man. He was constantly criticized by his father, and years later he was still very angry about it. As we talked through some of his sinful responses to the criticisms he'd received, he realized that his anger wasn't really at the people who spoke ill of his sense of style (he couldn't match pants and a shirt to save his life) or his folksy humor. Instead, he was angry at his hypercritical father. He admitted that he never felt affirmed by his dad and it made him angry. Every criticism would take him back to being ridiculed by the man who was meant to build him up.

The more we talked, the more he realized that much of his desire to serve as a pastor was grounded in the hope that his ministry might elicit some degree of affirmation from his otherwise cold and distant father. He would hear stories about how his "old man" would tell his coworkers that his boy was a "darn good preacher." Being a pastor made this man feel like he was able to finally earn his dad's approval and love. Shortly after realizing that his primary goal in leading a church wasn't to shepherd souls but to earn approval, my friend rightly began a process of phasing out of ministry.

Seeking Approval and Doing Penance

There is a never-ending stream of research that details the stresses and emotional wounds endured by a pastor during his tenure in ministry. However, to my knowledge, there has been no scientific study of the emotional wounds received prior to entering the ministry. In my experience, many pastors and aspiring pastors endured painful childhoods—either a lack of approval or some level of abandonment by their fathers. As I get to know aspiring pastors and those already in the pastorate, I now attempt to learn more about their family history. I ask about their background and inquire about its role in their pursuit of ministry. Every man I've pressed on this issue has admitted that his background, to varying degrees, played a role in his efforts to become a pastor.

Becoming a pastor because of your personal background is not wrong. God uses events and relationships to guide and shape us. But I've met a lot of men whose backgrounds have led them to serve in pastoral ministry for all the wrong reasons. In more than a decade of pastoral ministry, and nearly a decade in theological education, I've met some deeply wounded men who pursued the pastorate in order to achieve something "honorable" in life. Many men who become pastors do so because they are seeking validation and approval in response to a real or perceived lack of affirmation throughout their lives. The approval they experienced from older men in the church or from other pastors serves to soothe the ache of their hearts. Using the church to meet this kind of unmet emotional need is a soft form of spiritual abuse. If this is why you became a pastor, inevitably you will begin loving those who are meeting your needs and subconsciously despising those who do not. You will prioritize care for those from whom you feel you gain something and begin ignoring those who do not acknowledge their love for or value of you.

Similarly, there seems to be an endless supply of aspiring pastors who lived a raucous lifestyle before coming to Christ and want to make up for it by becoming pastors. This is less a zeal to let others know what grace has done in their lives and more a sense that they must atone for their past by "serving God" in full-time ministry. Every semester, it seems, I meet at least one student who was recently saved out of some kind of addiction or party-animal lifestyle and now wants to make sure he doesn't waste the rest of his life working a meaningless job. This impetus is largely based in a horribly naïve understanding of the doctrine of vocation.

At the heart of these motivations is the desire for validation, the belief that the role of pastor will help you know somehow that you are worth something. This reason for becoming a pastor is rabidly anti-gospel. Men who preach a scandalous gospel of grace—which declares we cannot earn God the Father's approval, and we shouldn't try, because Jesus has earned it for us in our place—are at the same time attempting to earn approval, whether it is from their earthly father or someone else. It's a sad and painful blind spot in their understanding of the gospel and its application to their own broken hearts.

When Jesus saves sinners, there is no disclaimer that they must make up for their sinful past. Rather, Jesus pays for our past and calls us to walk in obedience in the future. Far too many churches assume, and even teach, that men who have been radically converted should respond to grace by entering the ministry. On the contrary, in response to grace we ought to give grace. Grace carries with it no demand, but it does produce specific aspirations in life—sometimes including an aspiration toward pastoral ministry. Nevertheless, it is anti-gospel to assume that your salvation necessitates atonement for wasted years or a sinful past. It doesn't. Salvation is a work of grace.

My Struggle

My own background has led me to routinely wrestle through my motivations to discover if I am attempting to earn or prove anything by serving as a pastor. I can tell you that, at different points, I was attempting to do both.

I grew up in a region where the cultural norm for friends and families was one of restrained affirmation. That's not to say that every parent was unloving toward their children or that they always failed to provide encouragement. Mine certainly told me they loved me and they cared for me. However, the normal cultural ethic was largely grounded in the Appalachian mountain culture that permeated the area where I was raised (a culture that prizes strength and resilience). In such an environment that encourages toughness and hard work, displeasure is easily voiced and silence usually is meant to convey affirmation. Strangely, this regional approach to friendships and family life never made sense to me, even as a young child (maybe it's because of all the hugging and unrelenting encouragement I witnessed on the TV show *Full House* during my formative years). But it naturally inspired me to pursue "respectable achievements" that would cause my friends and extended family members to voice their approval. Additionally, for a variety of reasons, a few members of my family didn't carry a great deal of respect in the community, while some of my relatives were highly respected. I was driven by this "line of respectability," and I desperately wanted to be on the right side of it.

When Jesus redeemed me, I was burdened in that very moment to make his name known. I wasn't sure what that meant, but I assumed it meant some kind of pastoral ministry. So, from eight years of age onward, I told everyone that I desired to be a pastor. As soon as I entered my early teenage years, I realized that in my family's cultural milieu being a pastor guaranteed family pride. Therefore, dogmatic assertions of my "calling" would, on occasion, bring my family and friends to express pride and affirmation toward me. I liked it. Moreover, a young man who desired to pastor a church would certainly become part of the socially respectable branch of his family tree, right?

As I entered my adult years, I began to wonder what I was actually aspiring to. Pastoral ministry? Something else? Thankfully, during my late teens and early twenties, the Lord brought a number of mentors into my life who very bluntly confronted me over my motivations. They pressed hard to help me determine whether I was pursuing cultural and family affirmation or if I truly wanted to lay down my life for Christ's bride, the church. These men very directly called out some of my desires for approval and it changed my life. They told me that I had nothing to prove to God the Father. He already fully approved of me in Christ. It was the most freeing thing I'd heard in my young adult life.

Once I began to see myself and the gospel rightly, I was struck by the words of the children's song, "Jesus loves me." Some of my yearning to serve as a pastor was really an attempt to earn what I already had: Christ's love. The song that my heart was singing was not, "Jesus loves me, this I know," but rather "Jesus loves me, this I earn." What a horrible thing to believe, even if subconsciously.

I had superimposed on the Creator the hard-to-impress nature of some members of my family and our friends. I was attempting to earn the approval of my peers as well as my Heavenly Father. I was operating with an anti-gospel mindset. Here is the scandalous truth of the gospel: Jesus doesn't redeem achievers; he only redeems failures. God the Father doesn't exclusively love winners but losers. That's good news, because all that really exists are losers and failures. Yet because of my own sin and my background, my heart lied to me and made demands on me that Jesus never made.

Even now, my motivations are not always pure. In fact, I routinely expose the motivations of my heart to others in order to keep those motivations in check. I hope that if my reasons for serving as a pastor should ever become disqualifying that I would be told I need to step down.

What Are You Trying to Prove?

If I could sit down with every seminary student and aspiring pastor for one conversation, I would ask them: What do you want to achieve in ministry? Is there anything you are trying to prove to yourself or anyone else? Is there some sin from your past that you still experience guilt for—something that causes you to take on ministry tasks as an attempt to make atonement? If you never pastor a church that grows, how will you feel? What if you attempt to plant a church and it fails? What will your response be if your ministry is largely anonymous, without any books, blogs, conference invites, or respected titles? How you answer those questions will reveal a lot about why you are aspiring to be a pastor.

I think most guys know how they *ought* to answer those questions. But if you're honest with yourself and others, what would you really say? I've pastored churches that didn't really grow. It can be frustrating. Now I'm the pastor of a church that has grown steadily since we planted it a few years ago. If you think pastoring a growing church will make you feel like you've achieved enough to be satisfied, it won't. If you believe writing something that gains a wide audience will cause you to feel accomplished, you will be sorely disappointed. If you are convinced that earning a lot of degrees will enable you to look in the mirror and think, "I'm a respectable person," you'll wake up one day and realize you're still a bum. Just a bum with lots of student debt.

Whatever you are attempting to achieve for your own satisfaction or to earn the approval of others, pastoral ministry will not supply it. Whatever you may be attempting to atone for from your past, Jesus already paid for it. He doesn't need your pittance. At its core, all attempts to achieve in order to earn approval are grounded in anti-gospel assumptions. In Christ, you already have the only approval that matters.

Conclusion

If you enter the pastorate with a bent toward achievement for the sake of approval or accomplishments as a means of atonement, you will find neither. Furthermore, you will end up using and abusing the people under your care as you seek things you already have: approval and atonement.

My encouragement to all those in the pastorate is this: If you find yourself endlessly offended by the people in your church and continually dissatisfied by a lack of growth, notoriety, and so on, then you must check your motivations for being a pastor. The last thing the church needs is more men seeking to use the church to fulfill unmet emotional needs. Moreover, we only do damage to the fame of the name of Jesus when we stand in the pulpit and proclaim a gospel that we are not living.

For some, exposing the need to achieve will mean that you should stop aspiring to pastoral ministry (or resign from the ministry you are in). For others, as was the case with me, staring your own self-delusion in the face and seeing it for what it is will bring a renewed and rightly motivated desire to serve Christ as a pastor in the local church.

Regardless of the outcome of your wrestling with this lie, know this fact: If you have believed the gospel, you are already approved by the Father and your sins are atoned for by the Son. You don't have to be a pastor. You can do literally anything else and be just as approved by the Father and just as atoned for by the Son. Nothing changes that!

REFLECTION QUESTIONS

1. Is there some unmet emotional need that I am attempting to meet by being a pastor?

2. Do I assume that Christ will love me more if I'm a pastor?

3. Whose approval do I regularly seek with my pursuit of ministry or my accomplishments in ministry?

4. When am I most tempted to believe that God's approval of me is dictated by my position in the local church?

5. How does the work of Christ provide the remedy for my need to seek approval through achievement?

ACTION STEPS

1. Ask those closest to you to help you uncover any anti-gospel motivations for approval and achievement.

2. Make sure that you are regularly consuming books and sermons that remind you of the scandalous nature of the gospel.

3. Annually discuss your pursuit of achievement and approval with a biblical counselor who can help you see yourself rightly, through a gospel lens.

4

THE CALLED

"I'm called to be a pastor"

I was a fresh graduate from seminary, with a number of years of ministry already under my belt and an extremely high view of myself. I approached the senior pastor of the church where I had been hired recently and requested that I be ordained. He was excited and put together a council of pastors to oversee the process. We gathered across two meetings. The first was more or less a meet-and-greet, where I got to know the guys and they got to know me. The second was the formal interrogation that made me feel like I was being cross-examined in a military courtroom like Jack Nicholson's character in *A Few Good Men*.

Questions were coming my way left and right. Some were theological and others were more about ministry philosophy. I wish I could say that all my responses reflected wisdom and theological reflection. No, instead, I handled the barrage of inquiries with all the precision of a toddler attempting to put together a jigsaw puzzle. Still, I could sense that the room was on my side and that approval for my ordination was inevitable.

Then came the final question: "What if we say no?" My response was "I'll keep doing what I'm doing. Who are you to tell me what God has or hasn't called me to do?" I wish I had stopped there, but I didn't. I continued by pontificating about how the entire ordination process was meaningless. I was thoroughly convinced that one's calling was personal, subjective, and ultimately between that person and God. Additionally, I was convinced that the qualifications laid out in Scripture for elders were easily met the moment one experienced a subjective calling from God.

I was also sure the guys on my council felt the same way, and that they each would appreciate my response to their question. I was right. They affirmed my "call" to ministry and moved to ordain me as a pastor.

"Calling," the Bigfoot of the Bible

The problem for all of us gathered in that room that day was our unified conviction—no, our shared delusion—that a call to ministry is subjective, untestable, and comes from God himself. Sadly, once you embrace that lie, the next step is to utterly disregard what the Scriptures teach about biblical qualifications for elders. To be clear, I am not arguing that there is no such thing as a calling to pastoral ministry.[1] What I am saying is that much of the Protestant world has redefined "calling" to mean something it shouldn't: an

---

1. An excellent book that uses the traditional language of "calling" while making an effort to regain an accurate definition of what is meant by being "called to the pastorate" is Jason K. Allen's *Discerning Your Call to Ministry: How to Know for Sure and What to Do about It* (Chicago: Moody, 2016).

unfalsifiable sense that one has an irrevocable, God-given mandate for pastoral ministry. This notion of a subjective, private calling to ministry is like the mythology of Bigfoot.

Harry and the Hendersons was my introduction to the Bigfoot myth as a child. After watching the VHS movie we rented from the local Blockbuster store, I was convinced that I needed to find a Bigfoot of my own. Every time our family drove near a wooded area, I was on the lookout for my very own Sasquatch. Each time, I came up empty—until I at last found him! Not just any Bigfoot; I located Harry himself! I was walking through Kmart with my parents and I saw him. As we got closer, I found it odd that Harry was hanging out in the section with all the music cassette tapes. The moment we turned the corner I ran over to Harry only to find out that he was a cardboard cutout, and a bad one at that. They even got his name wrong: The bottom of the cutout said "Kenny Rogers."

How was I so convinced that something that doesn't exist *must* exist? Because I was five years old, and the lack of evidence was no obstacle for me. I wanted to believe, so I found evidence all over the place. I could not be convinced otherwise. As I matured, I came to realize that *Harry and the Hendersons* was a fantasy based on a popular and shared mythology. I've never seen Bigfoot. For the record, I have numerous friends who live in the Pacific Northwest, and they've never seen him either. Since I stopped looking for evidence, I realized that the evidence I had "seen" was subjective. It was no indication of the reality outside my own head, and it could have been interpreted in other, more accurate ways.

As soon as we make one's "call" to ministry subjective and remove serious consideration of the biblical qualifications for elders from the ordination process, madness ensues. It is this kind of mentality that provides platforms for heretics within gospel-preaching churches. It is this type of thinking that has destroyed the Protestant doctrine of vocation (because now ministry is a calling and every other job isn't). This approach to installing and affirming elders has led to the proliferation of unhealthy and unbiblical churches throughout the United States and the world. In the past two years, I have had the following three conversations with men who (along with their churches) had fallen victim to the calling mythology.

Conversation #1: A young pastor sat across the table from me, weeping. "Why is pastoral ministry so hard? I just want to quit! I hate it! I'm miserable!" He was in a less-than-healthy church, but I was still at a loss for why the situation he described was so crushing. I told him: "It is hard. It will be hard—and then you die and are forgotten." (My nickname should be Barnabas, the "son of encouragement.") I could have responded with something more uplifting, but I didn't want him to assume that merely changing his scenery would make pastoral ministry easier. He looked at me and said, "I know. It's just too much. Which is why I have to find comfort somewhere." He then went on to explain to me a series of secret sins he was indulging in to provide some release from the mounting stress and strain he was experiencing. These were not sins that simply needed to be fought so he could be faithful to his family and to his church. These were habitual, biblically disqualifying sins. As I pressed further and even encouraged him to quit, he fired back at me: "NO! I know I was called by God, and if I'm called by him I can't quit and nobody can tell me I must quit!"

Result: Soon after our discussion, his sin found him out and destroyed his family and left his church in shock. He was eventually fired and, even worse, the name of Jesus was marred. Sadly, just a few months later he began trying to re-enter the ministry because he was "called."

Conversation #2: I was catching up with a pastor I had known for years who played a huge role in my life. We hadn't talked much in a long time, and I could tell something was on his mind. I asked him how he was *really* doing. He confessed, "Terrible! The church is thriving, but things at home are bad. I'm not leading my family well at all." After about an hour of him detailing his family struggles, he said to me: "What would you do if you were me?" I told him I'd quit. I'd walk away from the ministry. If it was really destroying my marriage, harming my kids, and if I could no longer fulfill the scriptural qualification of managing my household well, I'd do something else with my life. His response: "I can't do that! God called me. This is my burden to carry."

Result: Now, almost two years later, he is desperate to leave the ministry to try and save his family. Still, he won't because he believes he must honor his "call" by God before honoring his calling to his family.

Conversation #3: As a professor, I have the privilege of meeting and investing in lots of students. It's one of the greatest joys of my life. Still, I hate conversations like this one. A zealous young man began meeting with me about his next steps in ministry. He was nearing the end of his degree program and was looking forward to his first opportunity in full-time ministry. I asked him if he was confident that he was ready for the pastorate. Looking incredibly perplexed, he said, "I mean, yeah. Why wouldn't I be? I have my degree. So I'm ready!" I quickly rephrased the question, "No, I'm not asking if you are prepared. Your degree tells the world that you've received training and you appear to be adequately prepared for the functional demands of pastoral ministry. What I mean is, do you believe you are biblically qualified or soon will be?" He had no clue what I was talking about. We opened the Bible and I showed him what I meant. I directed him to excellent resources like *Biblical Eldership* by Alexander Strauch and *Finding Faithful Elders and Deacons* by Thabiti Anyabwile. He willingly read them and then returned to meet me for coffee again. This time, his countenance was down and he was smoldering with rage. When I asked him, "Now, in light of what you've read, do you think you are qualified to pursue eldership right now? With anger and heartache in his eyes he said, "No! What is worse, I don't know if I can even trust pastors anymore. I'm years away from this. Years! But my pastor back home told me I was called. That I needed to be a pastor right away. That the Lord told him to tell me."

Result: Quite some time has passed and this young graduate is still struggling with the fact that he based several years of his life on what a pastor told him was a subjective calling from God. His confidence in the church is shaken, and he feels betrayed. It's truly a terrible thing, but he figured it out well before he assumed the pastorate in a church. Had he entered the ministry, the damage to his congregation would have been immense.

In order for churches to mature and guarantee they call biblically qualified men to serve as elders, we must move beyond this myth and embrace what the Scripture actually teaches. Rather than a subjective calling, the Scripture uses a different category and specific criteria.

Aspiring Men Wanted

I can't tell you how many pastors I've heard apply Psalm 105:15 to themselves (in the KJV: "Touch not mine anointed, and do my prophets no harm"). However, in context this verse is talking about the patriarchs Abraham, Isaac, and Jacob, calling them prophets as in Genesis 20:7. The trouble with applying this verse to pastors is that prophets and pastors are not the same thing. In his first letter to the young pastor Timothy, the Apostle Paul explains how a church ought to identify future overseers (elders, pastors): "The saying is trustworthy: If anyone aspires to the office of overseer, he desires a noble task" (1 Tim 3:1). Notice Paul doesn't say "if someone is called"; he says if they "aspire." I fear we have taken Old Testament language that refers to the calling of prophets and superimposed it on the office of elder.

Bobby Jamieson has said that a subjective call to ministry assumes two things. I really appreciate the way he explains these assumptions and their necessary conclusion:

Saying you're called to ministry presumes you think these two things about yourself: (1) you are, or soon will be, qualified to be an elder; (2) you are, or soon will be, sufficiently gifted in ministry that a church should pay you to do it. Unless you're talking nonsense, claiming a divine "call" has to imply both of these things—and it can't contradict either. But this reveals one potential problem with calling language right off the bat: if I say I'm called, who are you to contradict?[2]

The modern church has placed itself in a dangerous and unbiblical position by allowing the language of subjective calling to go unchecked. Instead, we must reclaim the biblical category of "aspiring."

When Paul refers to men aspiring to be elders, he is talking about their desire to serve the church in such a capacity. In 1 Timothy 3:1–7, Paul calls on Timothy (and the church) to examine and test the one aspiring, and he provides a similar test in Titus 1:5–9. Virtually every qualification that Paul supplies for the examination of a man aspiring to the pastorate has to do with character. Paul calls on Timothy to observe the man's moral restraint, his faithfulness to his wife, his conduct (both public and private), his treatment of his children, his handling of personal finances, and how he interacts with those around him. Nowhere does Paul mention a man's subjective calling. Nowhere! Additionally, he mentions gifting only once: "He must be able to teach." But note that this does not say a pastor must be a gifted and winsome communicator. Rather, Paul's concern is that he accurately communicates the content of Scripture.[3]

Gifting for teaching can be assessed rather quickly, even in one sermon. However, which of the other qualifications can be assessed quickly? None of them. In fact, this list

---

2. Bobby Jamieson, "The Double Presumption of Calling to Ministry," https://9marks.org/article/the-double-presumption-of-calling-to-ministry/.

3. For a detailed explanation of the way our church applies these qualifications as we assess potential elders, please see Appendix 1.

assumes a long period of examination. How long? I think that depends. Our church has an examination period of twelve to twenty-four months before we present an elder candidate to our congregation for affirmation. We have a very intentional process of assessment that simply cannot be expedited. While we may hire someone on our ministry staff while in the midst of this examination period, we will not vest them with pastoral authority until they have been thoroughly vetted and affirmed by our church body. We are convinced that the New Testament presents the pursuit of pastoral ministry not as a calling but as a process that leads to qualified and faithful shepherds caring for our church.

Conclusion

If the notion that a subjective calling is all you need to be a pastor is unbiblical, then there are many pastors who should quit. That may seem like an overstatement, but it isn't. We have far too many unqualified, untested men filling our pulpits and being vested with pastoral authority because they are gifted and believe they have been called to the ministry. We don't need more men who are gifted; we need more men who are qualified. We don't need more men who think they are called; we need more men who know they must patiently aspire while being tested and examined.

You may have entered the ministry believing God called you, and now you are desperate to get out. Can I tell you something scandalous? You can quit and it will not change your standing before God. If you're in Christ, your standing is secure.

I will take this a step further. If you take seriously what the Scripture says about qualifications and you realize that your ministry is built on a subjective sense of calling and that you are biblically unqualified to serve, then you should quit as soon as possible. You are attempting to undertake a work that will simply destroy you even as you destroy the congregation under your care. That doesn't mean you cannot aspire to pastoral ministry at a later time. It just means that you should be obedient to Scripture now.

Seminary students, do not believe for one moment that your degree qualifies you for pastoral ministry. It doesn't. It prepares you for the functional demands of pastoral ministry. Additionally, do not assume that a well-intended word of encouragement from a pastor or member of your home church is sufficient to qualify you for ministry. It doesn't matter what the oldest member of the church, the chair of deacons, or the senior pastor has said about your "calling." It matters what the Scriptures say about your qualifications. So, while in seminary, find a church that takes seriously what God has said and ask them to watch, test, examine, and assess your qualifications for eldership. Here is a pro tip: Virtually every qualification can be attainted through serious spiritual discipline.

Biblically qualified pastors, you are tired and worn out. I get it. I am too. You are growing tired of the mantra "life in them and death in me" as you sacrifice your life for a church that will rarely thank you. Rough stuff, isn't it? Listen to me: Get some rest. Take a vacation. Have brothers who are constantly encouraging you while pressing you to remain qualified, but don't quit. We need faithful, qualified shepherds. Still, if you find yourself just undone, know that there is no sin, no disobedience, and no harm in stepping down for a season. In fact, if you think you need to do so, then you probably do.

1. How have I been influenced by the idea that the call to ministry is a subjective feeling from God?

2. How thoroughly has my aspiration for ministry been tested?

3. How willing am I to have my sense of calling tested against the qualifications in Scripture?

4. For pastors: How do I evaluate potential pastors and elders?

ACTION STEPS

1. If you're already a pastor, put yourself under the scrutiny of other godly men to evaluate why you believe you are "called" to the pastorate.

2. If you are not a pastor, place yourself in a church that takes your aspiration seriously and that will hold you to what the Scriptures teach regarding biblical qualifications.

3. Be submissive to those to whom you've subjected yourself.

4. Seek the wisdom of biblical counselors as you assess the motives of your heart.

5

THE HOLY MAN

"My perceived holiness is more important than my pursuit of holiness"

I remind my congregation regularly that they are a collection of sinners. Even worse, their pastors are sinners. These reminders don't mean that any of us are free to wallow in our sinful inclinations, but we do have freedom to be open about our sin.

Most people who are visiting our worship gatherings, after reflecting on it for a moment, feel themselves put at ease by this admission. They begin to think, "If the pastor is broken, messed up, and sinful, then I can admit that I am too." They do not need to defend themselves or uphold a façade of sinlessness. In fact, this rhythm of honesty and confession has aided us in engaging ardent atheists, committed agnostics, and others who are visiting our worship gatherings with family or friends. They expect to hear a man who portrays himself as sinless railing against the sin of "you people" or the "sinners all around us," and they are put at ease when they discover this is not the case.

But for some newcomers to our church body, the introduction "Hey, I'm Dayton, I serve as lead pastor, and I'm a sinner redeemed solely because of Jesus in my place" is uncomfortable. Periodically I and other staff members will have someone approach us with a comment like, "I don't know if I could settle in here. I don't think I could be at a church where the pastor is a sinner." This is a complete misunderstanding of the gospel and of what Scripture teaches about human nature, yet it is widespread because of the myth of the pastor as holy man.

Dangers of the Holy Man Myth

Many Christians want to assume their pastor has a special connection to God, supernatural restraint, and a level of purity that makes him seem otherworldly. Many pastors (young and old) are not only willing to allow this holy man myth to continue, but even use it to their advantage. The constant pull in many Christian circles is for pastors to embrace the holy man mystique. Throughout my younger years, I knew only one pastor who admitted he was a sinful man rather than a holy man.

What is the danger in this? After all, at least in my tradition, most pastors who portray themselves as holy men attempt to make Jesus look big at the same time. Yet one problem is that when you portray yourself as sinless, or nearly sinless, you are inevitably bumping Jesus out of his rightful position as the Messiah (capital M) in order for you to play the role of quasi-messiah. If you desire for your church to envision you as largely sinless, you want them to view you in a way they should only view Jesus. As we fake our holiness, we are attempting to lay hold of glory that is not ours. In the end, a congregation that sees the pastor as a holy man who never (or rarely) sins will fail to realize that they really want Jesus. Instead, they will be willing for the pastor to serve as a cheap knock-off.

A second danger is that we begin to perpetuate inauthenticity regarding the confession of sin. The theologically minded and biblically literate members of your church know that you are a sinner. Still, if you present yourself as someone who doesn't struggle with sin, you are subtly modeling for the congregation a practice of hiding, concealing, or masking sin through a lack of transparency. The longer this continues in your public ministry, the greater decline you will see in genuine confession and repentance in your church body. When I meet a man in ministry who has difficulty with honesty regarding his sin, his struggles, and his failures, I know that his heart is yearning for the position that only Jesus can hold.

Last, when we allow the holy man myth to persist, we begin training our hearts to value perceived holiness more than the actual pursuit of holiness. As I prepared for ministry, I was told to make sure I exhibited the holiness of Christ before the watching eyes of a congregation. As a result, at different moments early in my ministry life, I found myself working hard to uphold my holy public image while giving no regard to the killing of sin in my private life. This was not only dishonest; it bordered on wickedness. When I became convicted over my embrace of this myth, I purposed to never again let myself fall into such a deception.

Disbelieving the Gospel

If being open about our sin is so beneficial for the life of our churches, why do so many pastors have such a hard time publically acknowledging their own sinfulness? I've found this hesitation to be grounded largely in pride and fear. We all want to be respected, and our pride leads us to wrongly assume that people will have less respect for a pastor who has to fight sin just like they do. Since we've so neglected the public confession of sin in the life of the local church, we are afraid it would be outright jarring to hear a pastor confess sin. Being aware of how fickle some congregations are, many men are afraid that breaking the ice by confessing their own sin will not just be uncomfortable; it will be career suicide.

On an even deeper level, what makes us susceptible to this pride and fear is our misunderstanding or perhaps momentary disbelief of the gospel. The gospel is the good news that God declares us righteous, his holy ones, not because of our performance but because of Jesus' performance in our place. The gospel frees us to fail because it tells us we already have failed and are accepted in spite of our failures. When we embrace the holy man myth, it's as if we forget the scandalous nature of the gospel. We wrongly assume that God has redeemed us by the work of his Son because he was unaware of our truly sinful hearts. We convince ourselves that admitting our struggles with sin may cause God to respond with, "Wait, what!? When I declared you righteous, I had no idea you would do that!"

Every time I'm tempted to conceal my sin, I'm comforted in my failures by a sermon that Charles Spurgeon preached on Jeremiah 32:

There can be no reason in the faultiness of the believer why the Lord should cease to do him good, seeing that *he foresaw all the evil that would be in us*. No wandering child of God surprises his heavenly Father. He foreknew every sin we should commit: he proposed to do us good notwithstanding all this fore-known iniquity. If, then, he entered into a covenant with us, and began to bless us with all our sin before his mind, nothing new can spring up which can alter the covenant once made with all these drawbacks known and taken into account. There is no scarlet sin which has been omitted; for the Lord has said, "Come now, and let us reason together: though your sins be as scarlet." He entered into a covenant that he would not turn away from us, to do us good; and no circumstance has arisen, or can arise, which was unknown to him when he thus pledged his word of grace."[1]

Pastor, preach the gospel to your own heart so that you have the freedom to confess sin to your people. Do not let your church assume that Jesus and you are near equals in possession of genuine holiness. You only bear the righteousness of Christ by imputation, not through your own actions.

How to Pursue Real Holiness

In addition to believing the gospel, pursuing genuine holiness (rather than its appearance) is the way to combat the

---

1. C. H. Spurgeon, "Perseverance in Holiness," in *The Metropolitan Tabernacle Pulpit Sermons*, vol. 35 (London: Passmore & Alabaster, 1889), 546–47 (italics original).

holy man myth. There are many excellent resources on what it means to pursue holiness, and what I have to say will not replace them. Instead, here are practical steps I take in my life, as a pastor, that I've found helpful in pursuing holiness and fighting the myth of the pastor as holy man.

First, I identify specific sins, the idols of my heart that I want to see die. One of the most amazing things to me is the initially evasive response I receive when I ask fellow pastors or seminary students, "What are some of the sins you are battling?" I don't think their evasion is intentional. Instead, it seems that many pastors and students are not in the habit of taking inventory of the sins they should be actively seeking to put to death. Yet I am confident that if I asked them about their spiritual gifts, the answers would come more quickly. All of us have taken one, two, or thirty questionnaires about spiritual gifts. Why the disparity? We would much rather celebrate the gifts we've been given than kill the sins we live in.

Second, I regularly confess sin to my wife and to other pastors. Confession isn't just the big stuff. It's not just when you're tempted to cheat on your spouse, embezzle money, or create a meth lab in the back of an RV. No, you and I must confess anger that no one knew about but us. Any hint of sexual sin should be confessed. A momentary flirtation with greed must be brought into the light. Why? If you are in the habit of confessing everything, you will be less tempted to hide issues that could cost you your marriage or ministry.

Third, make sure the church knows you are a sinner and regularly confess your sin to the church. I mentioned above one of my biggest safeguards against the holy man myth is regularly referring to myself, publicly, as a sinner.

And I do not merely tell my church family, "I'm a sinner"; I aim to make them aware of specific areas of sin I'm battling. For example, recently I've been transparent over my lack of confidence in God's sovereign plan. Since the day after our third son, Ransom, was born, we've experienced a pretty nasty car accident (and the ensuing medical issues for me and my children), a stream of unforeseen expenses (that would have financially drowned our family were it not for people jumping in to keep our heads above water), and a number of difficult ministry situations (including enacting church discipline). For nearly ninety days, we didn't go more than a week without a crushing expense, such as multiple appliances failing, or some kind of emotional hit.

It could be so much worse, and many people would call a difficult stretch like this a respite from their otherwise painful lives. But while I'm convinced that God is good and he is sovereign over all things, I have found myself battling anxiety and frustration over God's plan for and through this rough time. In the midst of this, a number of Scripture passages in our church's preaching schedule spoke directly to my heart issue. Thus, I made sure I told our church body of my momentary disbelief or lack of trust in God's plan.

The more I share about particular sins like this, the less I appear to be a holy man who is somehow beyond struggling with sin. In fact, if I ever adopted that persona, I would be immediately confronted. Also, when I preach of the scandalous nature of grace and how desperately we all need Jesus in our place, my church family knows I mean it—because they know how desperately I need it too. Finally, transparency from the pastor fosters a culture of confession where it's OK to admit your sin, but it is not

OK to conceal your sin. A gospel culture demands a practice of confession.

Here I need to supply a word of caution. You should not confess sin to the church with the same level of detail with which you confess it to other pastors or your spouse. Without a mutual understanding of the purpose of confession, your public openness could actually move from an encouraging and helpful practice to a destructive and distracting problem. Often, the only difference is *how* you publicly acknowledge your sin and the amount of detail you provide. We should never inadvertently glorify our sin or turn it into salacious fodder for lunch table discussions after the church service. There is a difference between confessing sin and purposefully aiming for the shock factor. So be open about your battles with sin, but be mindful of how you speak about them.

Conclusion

Any holiness that can be attributed to your name is only there because of imputation. You didn't earn it. You haven't been holy. You are not a holy man. Do not lie to the people in your care; tell them the truth! Tell them that you are a sinner. Make it a natural part of your pastoral prayer on Sunday mornings: "Lord, be with me, a sinner, as I preach your Word." The only holy man we want our churches to look to is the only Holy Man to ever live: Jesus.

REFLECTION QUESTIONS

1. Why is the notion of appearing to be a holy man so attractive?

2. How might I be allowing my congregation to assume that I do not struggle with the same temptations as they do?

3. What are some day-to-day rhythms I can adopt for confessing and addressing sin?

4. Is there an area of my life where I am more concerned with appearing holy than being holy? What changes can I make in this area to focus less on appearance and more on what is going on in my heart?

ACTION STEPS

1. Take an inventory of sin that you know is present in your life and that you desire to kill.

2. Establish a regular practice of confessing specific sins to your spouse and other pastors or elders.

3. Make it a regular habit to preach the gospel of grace to yourself, and seek out friends who will preach it to you as well.

4. In your next sermon, make clear that the only holy man you and your church should hope in is Jesus.

6

THE ANTI-FAMILY MAN

"I must sacrifice my home life for my ministry life"

I once had the pleasure of visiting one of the pastors I've most admired over the past decade or so. He is fairly well known in our area, and even though he is no longer in the pastorate, his reputation is one of an accomplished pastor and an excellent leader.

During our conversation in his study, I decided to peruse his library as he stepped away to make a phone call. On his shelves I noticed some pictures of him with his adult children, so when he returned I asked about his family life. His demeanor showed heartache, in contrast to the joyous way he had been answering my ministry questions. He shared with me how one of his children no longer professed faith in Jesus and how the others seemingly despised church life. When I asked him why, he said something like this: "For years, I prioritized the church family over my family. If I could do it all over again, I'd change everything. I became a successful pastor, but I was an unsuccessful husband and father."

I'm not sure where we ever got the notion that we must offer up our families on the altar of vocational ministry, but somewhere along the line this became a commonly held belief. At one point in my ministry life, I too believed that being faithful to Jesus in ministry meant sacrificing my family.

The exchange with that pastor has haunted me. The lesson I learned is that it is far too easy to put family life on autopilot while trying to achieve ministry success. In fact, it's even easy to rationalize sacrificing your family for the church because you're pursuing the redemption and sanctification of souls. This is utter foolishness.

The Lure of Busyness

Pastor, you are far busier than you ought to be. Maybe the church you shepherd has placed unrealistic expectations on you and your time, or maybe you've placed those expectations on yourself. It is possible that the people under your care want you to take the place of Jesus—and maybe you like taking the place of Jesus. Unlike the lie of the holy man, if you believe the lie of the anti-family man you may recognize your sinfulness, but it still feels good for people to demand from you what only Christ can provide. It feels good to have people look at you with the same needy eyes with which they should look toward Christ. It makes you feel important, needed, and valuable.

Perhaps you've also grown tired of ungratefulness from your wife or children. There is little thanks for how you serve them. Maybe your children have the audacity to act as if they don't need you. Maybe your wife doesn't sing songs of your praise as she once did; maybe she no longer responds to your preaching as though you were on par with George Whitefield, Billy Graham, and other great evangelists. In periods when you feel unappreciated, the lure toward busyness will be strongest.

Regardless of the root cause, if you are spending so much time on church matters that you are neglecting your home life, you are choosing the bride of Christ over your own bride. Hearing the demands of the church and responding to them with anything other than a humble appeal to your inability to take the place of Christ will leave your church disappointed, you exhausted, and your family in trouble.

Someone Else's Bride

Choosing the bride of Christ over your own bride might sound very high-minded, but the truth is that if you are married, your highest calling is not to be a pastor. Your highest calling is to be a pastor-husband and pastor-dad. If you are favoring the church over your family, the collateral damage from this dereliction will result in abandoning your shepherding duties to the most important flock you will ever shepherd. This flock will never number in the hundreds and they will never pay your salary, but they are your primary responsibility.

It is OK to resist the lure of spending all your time on church matters, because the church already has a groom and he is far better than you. Jesus gave his life to ransom his bride. He will take good care of her. He, not you, redeemed her. He, not you, is the guarantee of her salvation. It is not up to you to make sure everything gets done. Pastor, if you find yourself loving Christ's bride more than your own, or if you dedicate more time to discipling other people's children than to your own, you must repent and correct your course today. Immediately. Not tomorrow. Not next week. It needs to happen now! If not, then you are biblically disqualified from eldership and you need to resign, today. Any elder who places a higher priority on shepherding the church than on shepherding his family has disqualified himself from the pastorate (1 Tim 3:5).

If you are not a pastor yet and your highest romantic thoughts revolve around the church you will one day pastor rather than your future bride, disaster awaits you. In fact, you need to stay on the bench a while longer. Charles Spurgeon once advised a group of future pastors, "We ought to be such husbands that every husband in the parish may safely be such as we are. Is it so? We ought to be the best of fathers. Alas! Some ministers, to my knowledge, are far from this, for as to their families, they have kept the vineyards of others, but their own vineyards they have not kept."[1] In the short term, prioritizing the church may appear more urgent and more rewarding. But in the long term, prioritizing our families will produce greater fruit—both in our own families and, through our example, in others.

For those who are willing to admit their failure and who want to change course, let me encourage you that reprioritizing your life is not as huge of a task as it may seem. Instead, it's a matter of changing your rhythms and habits.

---

1. C. H. Spurgeon, *Lectures to My Students: Addresses Delivered to the Students of the Pastors' College, Metropolitan Tabernacle, Second Series*, vol. 2 (New York: Robert Carter and Brothers, 1889), 34.

Pastor-Husband

The gospel is the key to a happy and healthy marriage. For this reason, you and your spouse must regularly participate together in corporate worship, and you must engage in private worship/devotion as a couple. These are bedrock practices of gospel-driven obedience, and if they are not yet part of your life I suggest you adopt them immediately.

Still, even such spiritual disciplines are not enough to cause your wife to feel that she is loved and cherished with the same tenderness that Jesus cherishes his bride, the church (Eph 5:25–28). There are other habits and healthy rhythms that husbands and wives can adopt to cultivate stronger marriages. While I am not an expert on marriage, I am an expert on *my* marriage. Take my words as exhortations based on my limited experience and apply what is useful to your own situation. Here are just a few of the habits that have been beneficial in my own marriage:

Go to bed at the same time. I'm surprised by how many couples go to bed at different hours (though this is sometimes unavoidable due to outside factors like work schedules, if both spouses are employed). One of the best things you can do to encourage a "one flesh" mindset in your marriage is to go to bed when your wife goes to bed. When wives go to sleep and husbands stay awake watching TV or cruising the Internet, only trouble awaits. In a small way, routinely going to bed at different times creates the sense that each spouse is living a separate life.

Get the TV, smartphones, and computers out of your bedroom. I love technology more than most, so I understand how hard it can be to leave your iPhone in a different room. But if you find yourself needing to connect with other people on social media while laying next to your wife, something is off. You are missing out on valuable time to connect, talk, and pray together. The marriage bed should be a place of bonding, not a place to "veg out." One of the best rules we ever established in our home was to keep electronics out of our bedroom. The bedroom ought to be a sanctuary, a place for husbands and wives to shut the world out and focus on one another.

Assume the best about your wife. I regularly talk to ministry couples that are at odds. Too often, the heart of the problem is a lack of trust. Sometimes this battle with mistrust is related to sins from their past, but most of the time it is rooted in narcissism and self-centered attitudes. I have talked with couples who believe the other person purposefully leaves the toilet seat up or forgets to deadbolt the front door! If you assume the best about your spouse, you are far less likely to be in conflict. Your schedule is already so busy; don't waste valuable time with your wife by being in conflict.

Sacrificially serve your wife so she can assume the best about you. Make every effort to out-serve one another. Make it apparent that you die to yourself every day, for the good of your wife. Give grace and mercy as you pursue speaking only words of truth, love, and affirmation. Live a life that would cause your wife to assume the best about you.

Meet with a biblical counselor. If you commit to doing this at least yearly, it will do wonders for your marriage. You and your wife carry far more ministry baggage than you realize, and even just a few hours a year with a biblical counselor can help you keep your marriage healthy.

Speak only of your wife as beautiful. There ought to be some level of sacredness concerning the way you recognize your bride's beauty. This doesn't mean you never call your daughter(s) beautiful, or that when performing a wedding ceremony you cannot speak of the "happy groom and beautiful bride." But there will be periods in your marriage when your schedule will cause your wife to feel neglected. One way to affirm and privilege her place in your life is by refusing to speak of another woman as beautiful. Reserve this word solely for your wife. Cars are not beautiful. A jump shot is not beautiful. Your wife is beautiful, and that is the end of the matter. Also, memo to some pastors: Calling your wife "smoking hot" on social media (or from the pulpit!) is lame. Referring to her as "smoking hot" can be seen as objectifying her, while calling her beautiful honors her. As much as you can, reinforce her unique beauty by what you do or do not say.

Beyond adjusting your habits, you may find it necessary to change what you say to your wife. In the back of the popular book *The Five Love Languages* is a little quiz that helps you identify your love language.[2] Mine is "words of affirmation." When my wife tells me I'm a great husband and a good father, I feel loved. My wife is all about "acts of service." When I serve her, she feels loved.

If your wife's primary language is acts of service (or gifts, or quality time, or physical touch), don't lie to yourself and say, "Well, my wife's love language has nothing to do with words, so I'm good." Even though her primary

2. Gary Chapman, *The Five Love Languages: The Secret to Love that Lasts* (Chicago: Northfield Publishing, 2015), 191.

form of communication for love is centered on something else, there are things she needs to hear. In thinking about this, I've concluded that all wives—regardless of their primary love language—need to hear their husband say these five things:

- **"I love you."** Too often, a husband (me included) assumes that his wife knows she is loved. She doesn't. Over the years, I've sat with couple after couple who are in the midst of a difficult patch in their marriage. When I ask, "Tell me the last time you said 'I love you' to the other person," you'd be amazed at how many people cannot remember. Tell your wife you love her—regularly, daily, hourly.

- **"Thank you."** Being a wife and mother is hard work. If your wife is a homemaker, thank her for the hard and often-overlooked work of caring for your family. If you don't thank her, who will? If your wife works outside the home, thank her for the hard work of trying to accomplish two difficult tasks: earning an income and caring for you and the family.

- **"I'm not going anywhere."** One of the deepest needs every man can meet for his wife is providing a sense of security. You don't have to always say, "Hey, for the record, I'm not going to leave you." That could get weird and seem suspicious. Instead, periodically comment about the things you look forward to in future stages of life. On occasion, remind her that you are here to stay.

- **"I'm praying for you."** Even if I am praying for someone, I'm horrible when it comes to letting people know, including my wife. Pray for your wife and tell her you do. Let her know that when you talk to the most important Being that will ever exist (God), you mention the most important person in your life (your wife).

- **"You can have the remote."** I love my wife, but she loves some shows I don't. *Downton Abbey* nearly sent me into a depression; nothing about that show intrigued me. Still, she loved it, and it made her feel valued that I would endure each episode with her. Saying words like "we can watch what you want" isn't so much about the remote as it is about giving up your preferences for the sake of making her feel loved.

I encourage you to have an open and honest conversation with your wife. Ask her if she feels neglected, and how she would gauge the health of your marriage. Invite her to identify some things you can do to better cherish her and express love for her. It's not complicated! Simple, gospel-reflecting habits, along with some robustly masculine intentionality, are at the core of loving your wife well. Once you have ensured that you are shepherding your wife well, direct your attention to your children.

Pastor-Dad

Many pastors fail at being the pastor of their family. We may be ashamed to admit it, but often when we pontificate from the pulpit about how parents shouldn't outsource the discipleship of their children to the church, we aren't even discipling our own children.

Before you feel a heavy hand of condemnation, let me remind you that no man wakes up one day and instantly becomes the pastor of his home. It takes years of experience—and many awkward face-plants—to grow into that role. From my limited experience as a father and husband, here are a few simple habits that will get you on the trajectory to being a healthy "pastor-dad."

Pray for your family and with your family. It should be the most natural thing for a man to pray for his family, but it isn't. It takes intentionality. My wife is a praying woman, and her prayer life pushes me to have a healthier prayer life of my own. It is now part of my daily routine to pray for Rebekah and my boys. If you develop the habit of privately praying for your family, then publicly praying for them will come naturally. Your family needs to hear you pray for them. Your children need to hear their father praying for their salvation.

Turn off the TV, put down the phone, and engage. I've gone through periods when I struggled to come home from the office and simply be pastor-dad, not Pastor Dayton. Our culture calls us to take pride in maintaining a slammed schedule, but our culture also celebrates and encourages a million other things that starve our spiritual vitality and destroy our families. Don't come home from a long day and shut down. When you are with your family, turn off the TV unless you are watching it together. You also don't need to be checking sports scores or your email on your phone. I know it's hard, since many of us have rewired our brains to "need" to check our phones every few minutes. But it can wait.

Talk about Jesus with your family. What you talk about most often is what your kids think is most important to Dad. If you can't remember the last time you had a meaningful exchange with your family about the person and work of Jesus, then your kids have no idea that Jesus matters to you. You don't have to drop theology bombs on their little minds. Just talk to them about Jesus.

Read Scripture with your kids every night. There is no easier way to make sure you talk about Jesus than to read the book that's by Jesus and about Jesus. There are a number of great resources for families, and most of them can be used in increments of 10 or 15 minutes. For instance, if you have small children you can use resources such as *The Gospel Project Bible* or *The Jesus Storybook Bible*. Reading a chapter or two takes no time at all. The next day, come home from the office and ask your kids what they remember about the previous night's family devotion. Ask them how they applied the gospel truth from last night during their day. Tell them how you applied that truth to your heart and life. It's simple; it just takes intentionality.

Practice discipline that reveals the gospel. The vast majority of parenting advice from our culture is horrible. Why? Our nation has become post-Christian and is quickly moving toward being anti-Christian. Even for many who believe in God, the default worldview has become something akin to what sociologists Christian Smith and Melinda Lundquist Denton have called "moralistic therapeutic deism."[3] "Moralistic" means someone thinks God just wants them to be a good person; "therapeutic" means they think God wants them to be happy (according to their own definition of happiness); and "deism" is a way of saying God isn't personally involved in their life.

You do not want to tell your kids that Jesus matters and then parent them through a filter that encourages moralism. That duality is how you create little religious hearts

---

3. This term is from their book *Soul Searching: The Religious and Spiritual Lives of American Teenagers* (New York: Oxford University Press, 2005).

that try to earn God's favor by being good. This may be the most difficult aspect of being a father and a pastor. We face all kinds of real and perceived pressure to have children who behave properly, who obey, who do not become the stereotype of the wild and crazy pastor's kids. Our default wiring, with its natural inclination toward religion, will cause us to apply this pressure when disciplining our children, and in doing so will turn them into legalists.

If you believe the gospel, you will not be shocked by your child's sinfulness. You do not need to lament that your eighteen-month-old is a viper in a diaper the first time he disobeys, but you should remember that Scripture says we are sinners by nature. When we respond to our children's sin with shock, we communicate to them: "Do better, try harder, make yourself righteous." Our goal as fathers must not be mere behavior modification. Our aim is to see our children repent and believe the gospel. Therefore, do not respond to their sin in a way that simply calls for a change in behavior; respond in a way that calls for heartfelt repentance.

The moments when we discipline our children are of incredible value for pointing them to Jesus. I've found that asking my oldest son a few pointed questions keeps me calm and helps draw his attention to the Perfect Father in Heaven. I ask my son, "Who am I?" He says, "Daddy." That's right! "Do I love you, son?" He replies, "Yes!" I then tell him, "Because I love you, just as you are, please obey me." Sometimes it makes a huge difference. Many times, he doesn't get it. However, I'm trying to lay gospel groundwork, and that doesn't happen overnight.

None of this is hard. It just requires intentionality, yet we are often far too passive. This passivity is hurting your family. Begin implementing these basics habits now! As you pursue being the pastor of your home, you will fail. It's OK! We all fail, but we cannot allow failure to become defeat. The stakes are too high and your family is far too valuable.

Conclusion

I recognize that many pastors serve in churches where the culture is not very conducive to a healthy family life. There are programs every night of the week, and the pastor is expected to be at each one. It's hard. Therefore, I've tried to suggest rhythms that are doable for pastors who face crushing demands on their time.

But even though the rhythms of pastoring your family may require less time than you think, you need to fight against the lie that your family only gets what's left over after you've given your all to the church. Be clear in your own mind that your first priority is the flock that bears your name. If your church has expectations of you that are crippling to your family life, you need to speak up. If it falls on deaf ears, bring it up again. In the end, if the church culture demands a superman pastor who must attend every event on every night of the week, then you may need to serve elsewhere. The church may be looking to you as a Jesus substitute, and it may be necessary to leave for the sake of the church's health and yours. That's a decision you and your wife must make together, with wise counsel from others. It's a hard conversation to have, but for the sake of your highest callings (pastor-husband and pastor-dad), you must have it!

You fight against this lie by being faithful to your wife, by making her your priority instead of chasing Christ's bride. Shepherd the bride he gave you before you ever shepherd the bride he gave himself for, knowing that Jesus has called you to love her the way he loves the church. Shepherd your children. Tend to their souls. Make your discipleship ministry in your home the priority over the discipleship ministry in your church. The most important flock you will ever shepherd sleeps under your roof, sits on your lap, and has your eyes. Shepherd them first, even to the detriment of your ministry dreams and goals.

REFLECTION QUESTIONS

1. How am I tempted to prioritize the church over my family?

2. When was the last time I prioritized my bride over the bride of Christ?

3. Why am I tempted to tend to the needs of the church over the needs of my family? Is it rooted in my pride or my desire to be liked?

ACTION STEPS

1. Ask your wife to help you see your blind spots in shepherding your family. Specifically ask her when you are most prone to ignore the needs of your family.

2. When you get home from the office, put your phone away and just be with your family.

3. Have a direct and hard conversation with your church leadership about the need to prioritize your family.

7

THE CASTAWAY

"I'm the only one on this island"

Once upon a time, Tom Hanks was in seemingly every movie. Even if he wasn't the star of a film, he was in it! During that stretch, Hanks starred in *Cast Away* (2000), in which he survived a plane crash and was stranded on a remote island somewhere in the Pacific. One of the most memorable elements of the film was Hanks drawing a face on a Wilson-brand volleyball that had survived the crash. He befriended the volleyball and had conversations with it throughout the movie, aptly naming it "Wilson."[1]

Hanks's friendship with this inanimate object serves as a reminder that all human beings desire relationships. In fact, one of the ways we most clearly reflect the image of God is our innate longing for relationships. God

---

1. As of this writing, you can still buy a replica of the "Cast Away Volleyball" from Wilson's website—in case you, too, are looking for a friend: www.wilson.com/en-us/volleyball/balls/outdoor-volleyball/cast-away-volleyball.

is a perfect community of divine relationships within his triune nature of Father, Son, and Spirit. Thus, the human desire to have meaningful relationships reflects our longing to be like our Creator.

Since relational desires and interactions are intrinsic to human nature, it ought to strike us as odd that so many pastors are relatively friendless. That's not to say that pastors are disliked or uncared for. On the contrary, pastors are generally loved and well-known. However, most pastors I know suffer from extreme feelings of loneliness. Many believe that outside of their ministry acquaintances who pastor other churches, they are truly friendless. Now, I doubt there are many pastors turning to volleyballs for friendship (although I did know a pastor who called his KJV Bible "James"). However, few feel they have someone who knows them intimately.

As I've talked with other pastors and asked about their sense of loneliness, I've found a common denominator: We had all been given the terrible advice that we should keep our distance from the congregation. That's not to say we shouldn't know about their lives, but it means they shouldn't see us as one of them; otherwise, we risk losing their respect. After all, if people know how overwhelmingly normal their pastor is in everyday life, how can they can view him as an authority figure who communicates the word of God? Moreover, sheep bite if you get too close. Therefore, longevity in the ministry of shepherding necessitates avoiding too many wounds from the flock.

During my first few years in ministry, I followed this advice and it made me miserable. The pastors I know who struggle with finding meaningful friendships have all told me the same thing. We each pursued living our lives on an island. We were proverbial castaways, and we did it to ourselves on purpose. We told ourselves that common Christians need community, relationships, and friends, but pastors do not. This is a lie that denies our own humanity, God's triune nature, and our bearing of the image of God.

With Friends Like These ...

Living your life on an island is dangerous. It's destructive. It is deadly to your soul. When you have no friends, you have no accountability. When there is no accountability, even the most spiritually mature will fall into deep sin. It's inevitable.

You also need friends in the church to avoid sinning against the church. If you never develop emotional bonds in the church, you will never love the church. If you do not love the church, you will be more inclined to use and abuse the church for selfish gain (e.g., purely for a paycheck or for building your own platform).

Additionally, as pastors we ought to constantly call our church family to meaningful engagement in the kind of community created by the gospel. In the early chapters of Acts, we find the believers living life together. How can we call the church to eat, work, and play together if we are not doing the same? Throughout Acts you never see the apostles and early church leaders separating themselves from the everyday lives of the believers. Rather, they lived in constant relationship with one another. For instance, Paul lived with and worked alongside Priscilla and Aquila (Acts 18).

It's hard to be more relationally intimate with someone than living in their home, working with them each day, and shepherding their soul. Yet this is exactly the kind of pastor-to-congregant relationship we find in the New Testament. Is it messy? Yes! Does it lead to potentially hurt feelings? Just ask Paul how he felt about John Mark when he left him hanging (Acts 15:37–39). There were some deep wounds there and relationships that took years to mend (Col 4:10; 2 Tim 4:11). Still, time and again we find Paul planting churches and living his life, intimately, with those he pastored.

Forming friendships in the church does not make you immune from problems. The first time I broke with the advice to live on an island, I developed a strong friendship with a man in a church where I served as one of the pastors. This guy was older than me, accomplished in life, and yet he wanted me not only to be his friend but to disciple him. I'd like to say it was the best thing to ever happen to me in ministry, but it wasn't. I befriended this man. Loved him. We kept up with one another after I moved away to serve another church. Still, he ended up concealing from me secret sin that eventually led to the dissolution of his marriage. I felt betrayed, like I never knew him at all.

I wish that was the only sad story I had to share, but it isn't. Since that first attempt, I've made many, many friends in the churches I've pastored. And I've been lied to, betrayed, gossiped about, maligned, and offended. But the very worst experience was having to oversee the formal church discipline of people I've called my friends. That involved a deep pain I cannot even begin to prepare other pastors for. It is the horrible, grisly, terrible side of befriending church members—the danger I was warned about.

In fact, one of the objections to pastors befriending a church members is that they will be unable to pursue church discipline for friends who fall into unrepentant sin. However, I believe my friendship caused me to pursue this person with even more intentionality than I otherwise would have. Yes, it made discipline more painful. But I've found that, even with this kind of pain, the blessings, joys, and gifts of grace inherent to friendship within the local church far surpass the liabilities.

The Joy of Friendship

In contrast to the lie that you need to keep your distance to be a pastor, some of my best friends are in the church I pastor, and their friendship has made me not just a better pastor, but a better man. Many of my friends are very different from me. Some of them are hunters; I prefer to hunt in the meat aisle of my local Harris Teeter. Some of them are motor heads; I get my oil changed at WalMart. One of my friends is even a Hollywood stuntman; I don't like climbing up anything higher than a stepladder. Yet these relationships have shown me three insights about pastoring I would've missed if I had stayed a castaway.

First, pastoring is more than catechizing a group of people with good doctrine.[2] It's about exemplifying the implications of good doctrine for all of life. Most of the time I spend with my friends in the church is not spent talking doctrine and books. Instead, we are doing seemingly "unspiritual" things and talking about everyday life.

---

2. While pastoring is more than catechizing a congregation, it is not less than that. If the word "catechism" seems foreign to you, let me explain. A catechism is a simple Q&A-style plan to instruct your people in sound doctrine and biblical truths. We use these in our church body, and I recommend you employ them in your church as well. For more information, see my book *Church History for Modern Ministry* (Bellingham, WA: Lexham Press, 2016).

Nevertheless, as all good theologians know, everything for the believer is a spiritual activity, no matter how "unspiritual" it may seem. Therefore, some of my most important shepherding involves living life alongside these men and helping them see gospel implications in routine areas of life.

Second, you cannot shepherd people you do not know. My preaching and teaching are light years better than they used to be, primarily because I know where the hearts of the people are in terms of obedience to Scripture, temptation, and the pressures of culture. And it's not just that I can speak with greater specificity about things that I know are affecting people; it's that I can speak more naturally. I used to have a very strong "preacher voice." We've all seen and heard the pastors who sound like Jim Gaffigan in casual conversation, but the moment they step behind the pulpit their voices and speaking rhythms mirror those of the late Adrian Rogers—booming and authoritative, with a dash of Southern sing-song rhythm. I can truly say I don't do that anymore. I know my church intimately, and I approach the pulpit that way. I know these people. They know me. So I talk to them on Sunday mornings in the same way I speak to them during the week—just louder and with more hand gestures. (I'm an extreme hand-talker; it looks like I'm directing air traffic when I preach.)

Third, friends in the church keep you from quitting. After a brutal Sunday, a long week, repeated confrontations of someone's sin, or a streak of shepherding through tragedy after tragedy, it's only natural to want to quit. If you don't have meaningful relationships within the church body, you probably will quit. It's hard to continually lay down your life for the good of people you aren't emotionally invested in.

One of the best encouragements for me is my small group. When I've been going through a difficult period of shepherding—whether it be because of biting or wandering sheep, or fighting too many wolves at once—I know that my group will remind me why I do what I do. The reason is that these are my friends. They are family. Yes, it's hard, painful, and sometimes thankless service, but I am regularly reminded that I'm doing it for people I know and love—and I am serving people who know and love me in return. I can't quit just because I'm beat up or worn down. In fact, because they know me and we are friends, I can tell them I'm beat up and worn down.

A Word of Caution

Having close friends in the local church is biblical, affirming, and freeing. Still, there are some significant dangers that come with seeking out friendships in a church you pastor. As you seek to move away from the lie of the castaway, you must be as discerning with your friendships in the local church as you would be anywhere else.

First, recognize that there are people in the church who will want to be your friend for purely selfish reasons. You should not engage in a deep friendship with everyone who pursues one with you. On many occasions, I've met men who desperately wanted a friendship with me not because of who I am as a man, but because of what I do as a shepherd. Their assumption was that by befriending me they would have a seat at the table of influence. Others pursued me because they wrongly believed that by being friends with the pastor they would have a special connection to Jesus. They didn't know that I have no more of a direct line to the Messiah than any other believer. Be on guard for attempts at relational extortion.

Second, be aware of your human tendency to play favorites. You will want to give your best friends preferential treatment. Don't do it. If you do and you are called out for it, repent and apologize. Even though you will naturally be closer to some than others, always remember that you are the pastor of the entire congregation.

Finally, while in this chapter I have countered the lie of the castaway by telling you to cultivate friendships in your church, you may need to do more. In addition to seeking friendships in your congregation, you should also seek meaningful friendships with other local pastors. Those who are actively shepherding churches can immediately identify with the unique challenges of a pastor's lifestyle. In his memoir *The Pastor,* Eugene Peterson writes about the importance of a regular gathering called the Company of Pastors that he met with for twenty-six years while pastoring a church in Maryland. Each week, a member of the group would take a passage from the Bible and give "an exegetical orientation in the text, along with homiletical suggestions that then led into conversations on ways of being a pastor in sanctuary and homes and community throughout the week. ... Our agenda was our vocation as pastor in the actual conditions of our workplaces, our congregations."[3] Meeting with pastors of other churches can help

---

3. Eugene Peterson, *The Pastor: A Memoir* (New York: HarperOne, 2011), 148.

you feel less alone, and it can foster greater cooperation between churches.

Conclusion

You were created for relationships, and your office as a pastor doesn't change that fact, nor should it. The job you have before you is to point your people to Christ and exemplify the character of Christ. Jesus was universally recognized not just as friendly, but as having friends (John 15:15). You cannot shepherd in a way that mirrors the Good Shepherd unless you are a shepherd with friends. You will not leave the ninety-nine to pursue the one if you do not know the name or care about the life of the one lost sheep. You will not stare into the face of wolves and be willing to shed your own blood to protect sheep you do not love. You cannot survive as a shepherd if you're afraid the sheep will bite, and you cannot survive on an island if you're a castaway.

REFLECTION QUESTIONS

1. How have I been influenced by the idea that pastors must not get too close to their congregations?

2. How can I cultivate more meaningful relationships within my congregation while avoiding the dangers of false motives or favoritism?

3. A shepherd who knows the members of his congregation will easily be able to recount their needs based on meaningful interaction with them. What pressing needs am I aware of because of the intimacy in my relationships? (Take a moment and list some of the needs.)

4. How many recent conversations, marked by vulnerability, have I had with members of my church?

ACTION STEPS

1. Begin building a genuine friendship with a man (or men) in your church.

2. Avoid making every exchange with your church members about the "formal" business of the church. Instead, go fishing, go to a game, have them over for dinner. Just be a friend.

3. Identify areas where you are unwilling to be vulnerable and make a conscious decision to pursue vulnerability.

4. Designate a monthly block of time to meet and be open with another pastor in your community.

8

CONCLUSION

The Invention of Lying

Pastor, you believe lies. You tell lies. You tell yourself lies. Like every human being, you are quick to recognize lies that others are believing and telling themselves, but you are slow to recognize the lies you tell yourself.

You preach and teach Scripture, so you know the story of how lies began. In Genesis 3, the serpent slithers into the garden and begins tempting Eve through a series of questions. He asks her what God said about the trees of the garden, and she replies with this: "We may eat of the fruit of the trees in the garden, but God said, 'You shall not eat of the fruit of the tree that is in the midst of the garden, neither shall you touch it, lest you die' " (Gen 3:2–3). In response, Eve is told that God's command about the tree isn't meant to protect her, but to protect God from her and her husband. So the fall begins with a lie about God—that he does not love Eve or have her best interests in mind. Eve then believes a lie about herself—that she can take God's throne if she just eats from the tree (Gen 3:4–5). Human pride leads us to believe lies about God, which in turn leads us to believe lies about ourselves.

The deception in the garden becomes even worse when Adam refuses to counter the serpent's lie with the truth. He knows that all of this is untrue, yet the moment Eve is deceived and eats the fruit, Adam joins in. While Eve is misled, Adam *chooses* to believe what he knows is a lie—and his decision ends up being the match that lights the world on fire. The world's first spiritual leader—the man whose God-given role in the garden is described using the same Hebrew words that define the work of Israel's priests (spiritual leaders)—completely blows it through his refusal to counter a lie with the truth. You and I are still suffering from the wreckage he caused. Our world is still on fire. Our hearts our still aching, and our bodies are still failing. When those responsible for the souls of others choose to believe lies, they cause widespread damage that echoes through the ages.

We all need to hear the story of the first sin again, because we're prone to forget what it means. We recognize that every lie we've discussed in this book is, in fact, a lie. Yet we find it easier to embrace lies than to resist and expose them. Adam's willful embrace of what he knew to be a lie ruined God's good creation. And your willful embrace of lies will ruin your family and the church you shepherd.

How do we avoid falling prey to the lies pastors believe? By acknowledging that we are Adam: We sin like Adam, and we need the same remedy that Adam needed. We need to tell the truth to ourselves about who God is, who we are, and what we need.

The remedy is foreshadowed and promised in Genesis 3. After our first parents throw the creation into a cycle of sin and death, they run and hide from God (Gen 3:8). They hide behind the trees in an attempt to protect themselves from the wrath of God against their cosmic treason. Pastor, we run to the same place today to be saved from God's righteous wrath against our sin—a tree. The tree we run to is the tree where Jesus died in our place.

Action Step #1: Acknowledge, once again, your desperate need for Jesus in your place. Preach the gospel to yourself. Remind the man you see in the mirror every morning that you too are a liar who loves to believe lies, and it's only Jesus in your place, on a tree, that saves you from wrath.

God calls to Adam and Eve in the garden, and Adam steps out from behind the trees. Here is his moment. God knows what has happened, yet he gives Adam the opportunity to own it, to plead for forgiveness. Instead, Adam blames Eve and blames God for creating Eve (Gen 3:12). Pastor, throughout Scripture, one of the markers of biblical manhood is that a man is willing to take responsibility, even for his sin. Adam passes the buck and shifts the blame.

Action Step #2: Acknowledge that you believe lies and that your lies (whether told or believed) have done incredible damage to you, your family, and your church. Take responsibility for any wreckage your lies have caused.

We expect God to respond to Adam with crushing ferocity, but he doesn't. Instead, God curses the serpent and gives Adam and Eve the hope of the gospel. God promises that a son will be born who will crush our enemy (Gen 3:15).[1]

---

1. This passage is often referred to as the *protevangelium*, or "first gospel," and may be alluded to in such New Testament texts as Luke 10:18–19 and Romans 16:20.

A hero will come and fix what we've broken through our lies (both told and believed).

Action Step #3: Rest in grace. Make Jesus the hero of your life and the hero of your ministry. Point your family and your church toward Jesus.

Our entire ministry, to our family and to our church, must be pursued in light of the fact that we are Adam, and we are pointing the world to the second Adam promised in Genesis 3:15. We need to remind ourselves daily of this. Too often we think of ourselves as teachers who have heard it all before. Yes, we are teachers, but we are learners first and must remain learners. We are leaders who point others to Christ, but we ourselves must first be followers of Christ. If we are not constantly reminding ourselves why we need Christ, it can be easy to forget why others need him too. The moment we lose sight of who we really are—sinners in need of Christ—is the moment we begin believing lies.

APPENDIX 1

ELDER QUALIFICATIONS

I f anyone aspires to the office of overseer [elder/pastor], he desires a noble task" (1 Tim 3:1). This means that anyone serving as an elder must *desire* to serve as an elder. By implication, this means his wife must affirm this desire and share in his burden to shepherd the church body. She must be open to him serving in a capacity that could lead to pain and suffering, great demands on his time, and intense levels of scrutiny and criticism.

But we saw in chapter 4 that a mere burden or sense of calling is not enough to qualify a man to serve as an elder. Paul follows up the above statement with a list of qualifiers, and the process of identifying and establishing an elder demands a thorough investigation into whether a candidate meets these biblical qualifications. It may sound shocking, but biblical qualifications for eldership often receive little more than a cursory glance from a church body, church leadership, or a man desiring to be an elder. A church body falls into great error when anyone feeling "called" to serve as a pastor is affirmed in that calling without thorough examination.

Below you will see the biblical qualifications of an elder as listed in 1 Timothy 3:1–7 and Titus 1:6–9, along with a practical outworking of each qualification. Our church uses this guide to explain what we are looking for in the life of a man who aspires to the office of elder.

None of this is groundbreaking. If it were, we'd be in danger of creating our own extrabiblical qualifications for eldership. Instead, this guide is adapted and summarized from the work of Benjamin Merkle,[1] John MacArthur,[2] Thabiti Anyabwile,[3] and Alexander Strauch.[4] We have found this material incredibly helpful in the early stages of identifying a potential candidate (and his wife) to begin working through the eldership process.

1. Above reproach (1 Tim 3:2; Titus 1:6)

- He must be an exemplar of biblical manhood.
- He must live his life in such a way that it would be difficult to ever accuse him of wrong doing in his private life, married life, or career life.

2. The husband of one wife (1 Tim 3:2; Titus 1:6)

- He must be a "one-woman man."

---

1. Benjamin Merkle, *Why Elders?* (Grand Rapids: Kregel, 2009), 65–81.
2. John MacArthur, *The Master Plan for the Church* (Chicago: Moody Press, 1991), 215–33.
3. Thabiti Anyabwile, *Finding Faithful Elders and Deacons* (Wheaton, IL: Crossway, 2012), 51–103.
4. Alexander Strauch, *Biblical Eldership* (Colorado Springs, CO: Lewis & Roth, 1995), 67–84.

- He must be committed to his wife (if he is uncommitted to her, he will be uncommitted to the bride of Christ).
- He must not be unfaithful to his wife physically.
- He must not be unfaithful to his wife emotionally.
- He must not be lustful over other women (i.e., he must not consume pornography or sexually enticing material). This is very serious. When examining a man, steps must be taken to ensure he is not consuming such material. Questions should be asked about movies he watches and other media content he regularly consumes.
- He must not be unfaithful to his wife by directing all his time and energies into his career, hobbies, or ministry.

3. Sober-minded (1 Tim 3:2)

- He must be a clear thinker.
- He must be able to clearly articulate difficult biblical concepts.
- He must consume good biblical content for the sharpening of his mind.
- He must have largely settled in his own mind many of the big theological questions of our day (i.e., election and predestination, the nature of the church, the Trinity, the incarnation, his overall theological system).

4. Self-controlled (1 Tim 3:2; Titus 1:8)

- He must exhibit a mind and lifestyle driven by the Scriptures and logical thinking.

- He cannot be driven by his emotions or given to emotional outbursts.
- His lifestyle and track record must demonstrate strong decision-making abilities.
- He cannot exhibit a haphazard record in his employment history. This means that if he has a history of short periods of employment with one company or another, there may be concerns (but obviously there can be mitigating circumstances involved).
- He must demonstrate self-control in his ministry service. If there is a consistent record of jumping from one ministry capacity to another, this could be a concern.
- He must not be impulsive in his finances.
- He must demonstrate a lifestyle of common-sense thinking, particularly in areas of life management (family life, financial life, and career life).

5. Respectable (1 Tim 3:2)

- He must exhibit an attitude of taking responsibilities seriously.
- He must manage his time well (i.e., he must not often be late and/or unprepared).
- Others must take him and his wife seriously.
- Others must think his advice carries weight.
- He must back up his words with actions and follow-through.
- His life must exhibit signs of orderliness and self-discipline.

6. Hospitable (1 Tim 3:2; Titus 1:8)

- He uses his home as a base for ministry.

- He is cheerful, gracious, and kind.
- He makes a visible effort to reach out to new people and make them feel comfortable.
- His wife also does the above.

7. Able to teach (1 Tim 3:2; Titus 1:8)

- He can clearly communicate the teachings of Scripture.
- He must exhibit a lifestyle of discipleship.
- He must be known for using the Scriptures in calling the lost to faith.

8. Not a drunkard (1 Tim 3:3; Titus 1:7)

- He uses his Christian freedom wisely.
- He has not allowed any sin to master him.
- He is not addicted to any mind-altering substance, whether legal or illegal.

9. Not violent but gentle (1 Tim 3:3)

- He is able to maintain visible Christian love for those who have personally offended him or attacked him.
- He is a peacemaker.
- His life is not filled with "drama" of any kind.
- He handles criticism well.
- He "lets things go" after they have been resolved.

10. Not quarrelsome (1 Tim 3:3)

- He does not argue with those in authority over him (his pastor, his boss, and so on).
- He demonstrates a teachable spirit.
- He is gracious toward people he disagrees with.
- His presence promotes unity, not disunity.

11. Not a lover of money (1 Tim 3:3; Titus 1:7)

- He does not exhibit a greedy heart.
- He is not willing to compromise his convictions in order to benefit financially.
- His service to the church is not motivated by financial gain.
- He gives generously of his financial resources to the church.
- He values ministering to people more than the idea of holding a paid position at a church.

12. Manages his own household well (1 Tim 3:4; Titus 1:6)

- He possesses organizational abilities.
- He manages the affairs of his family well.
- He has a good financial plan for caring for his family.
- He maintains a budget in his home.
- His wife respects him and speaks well of him publicly and privately.
- He leads his home spiritually.

13. Keeps his children submissive (1 Tim 3:4; Titus 1:6)

- His children respect him.
- He does not have adult children living in his home who are unbelievers in rebellion.
- His children's lives exhibit evidence that he is a loving father.

14. Able to care for God's church (1 Tim 3:5)

- He possesses life-management and organizational abilities.

- His life is not in disarray.
- He exhibits the ability to manage his own life, household, budget, family, career, and so on.

15. Not a recent convert (1 Tim 3:6)

- He has a faith that has been tested over time.
- He has, over a period of years, produced fruit that demonstrates regeneration.

16. Well thought of by outsiders (1 Tim 3:7)

- The unbelievers in his life respect him and his family.
- He is honest in his personal dealings.
- His social life reflects gospel centrality.
- His neighbors think well of him.

The remaining qualifications are those found in Titus 1:6–9 that do not have a direct parallel in the 1 Timothy passage.

17. Not arrogant (Titus 1:7)

- He is a "team player" in carrying out the mission of the church.
- He does not desire to serve as an elder because of any perceived entitlement to that role.
- His motivations to serve as an elder reflect a burden to shepherd hearts, not a desire to have a title.
- He asks for advice in making decisions.
- He is teachable.

18. Not quick-tempered (Titus 1:7)

- He is not driven by his emotions.
- He demonstrates control of his emotions, even in stressful situations.

- He is quick to forgive.
- He does not punish his children in anger.

19. Lover of good (Titus 1:8)

- He loves things that point to Jesus.
- He has an optimistic view of life because of the gospel.

20. Upright (Titus 1:8)

- He deals fairly with people.
- He is willing to make a difficult but godly decision, even if it will bring criticism.

21. Holy (Titus 1:8)

- He exhibits a strong prayer life.
- He pursues Christlike holiness.
- He has a healthy diet of Scripture in his private life.
- He puts to death the sins in his life.

22. Disciplined (Titus 1:8)

- He accomplishes tasks on time.
- He is dependable.
- He arrives to meetings and appointments on time.
- He manages his time well.

23. Able to give instruction in sound doctrine and rebuke those who contradict it (Titus 1:9)

- He can defend biblical doctrine.
- He shares the same theological understanding as the teaching/preaching pastor.
- He has a solid understanding of the "big picture" of the Scriptures.

APPENDIX 2

RECOMMENDED READING

One of the most important things a man who is aspiring to pastoral ministry can do is read. First, read the Scripture. You must love and know the Bible well if you are to serve the church of Christ. Second, you must consume resources that will help equip you for pastoral ministry. Here are some suggested books for those aspiring to pastoral ministry.

Biblical Eldership

It is easy to assume that we know and understand what a pastor/elder/overseer is in a biblical sense. However, the biblical teaching on elders and their qualifications is often at odds with what is found in many local churches. Therefore, aspiring pastors must study what Scripture actually teaches regarding elders. These books lay out well what biblical eldership looks like in a modern context.

- Thabiti Anyabwile, *Finding Faithful Elders and Deacons* (Wheaton, IL: Crossway, 2012).

- Benjamin L. Merkle, *40 Questions About Elders and Deacons* (Grand Rapids: Kregel Academic, 2007).
- Benjamin L. Merkle, *Why Elders? A Biblical and Practical Guide for Church Members* (Grand Rapids: Kregel, 2009).
- Phil A. Newton and Matt Schmucker, *Elders in the Life of the Church: Rediscovering the Biblical Model for Church Leadership* (Grand Rapids: Kregel, 2014).
- Jeramie Rinne, *Church Elders: How to Shepherd God's People Like Jesus* (Wheaton, IL: Crossway, 2014).
- Alexander Strauch, *Biblical Eldership: An Urgent Call to Restore Biblical Church Leadership* (Colorado Springs, CO: Lewis and Roth, 1995).

For a book that uses the more traditional language of "calling," this is a great resource:

- Jason K. Allen, *Discerning Your Call to Ministry: How to Know for Sure and What to Do about It* (Chicago: Moody, 2016).

Family Life

Just as pastoral ministry places unique demands on the pastor's leadership abilities, it also results in unique family dynamics. Those aspiring to ministry ought to be intimately familiar with the goal of Christian parenting and marriage. Additionally, you must be prepared for the unique aspects of Christian family and marriage within the context of pastoral ministry.

- Ajith Fernando, *The Family Life of a Christian Leader* (Wheaton, IL: Crossway, 2016).
- Gloria Furman, *The Pastor's Wife: Strengthened by Grace for a Life of Love* (Wheaton, IL: Crossway, 2015).

- Timothy Keller, *The Meaning of Marriage: Facing the Complexities of Commitment with the Wisdom of God* (New York: Dutton, 2011).
- Tedd Tripp, *Shepherding a Child's Heart* (Wapwallopen, PA: Shepherd, 2011).
- Donald S. Whitney, *Family Worship: In the Bible, in History, and in Your Home* (Wheaton, IL: Crossway, 2016).
- Timothy Z. Witmer, *The Shepherd Leader at Home: Knowing, Leading, Protecting, and Providing for Your Family* (Wheaton, IL: Crossway, 2012).

Holiness

One of the keys to a fruitful life in pastoral ministry—and to Christian life in general—is the pursuit of holiness. At the same time, it is imperative that we acknowledge we are not "holy men." These resources will help you understand what holiness is and what practices facilitate the pursuit of holiness in one's life.

- Jerry Bridges, *The Pursuit of Holiness* (Colorado Springs: NavPress, 2006).
- Kevin DeYoung, *The Hole in Our Holiness: Filling the Gap between Gospel Passion and the Pursuit of Godliness* (Wheaton, IL: Crossway, 2012).
- J. I. Packer, *Rediscovering Holiness: Know the Fullness of Life with God* (Grand Rapids: Baker, 2009).
- J. C. Ryle, *Holiness: Its Nature, Hindrances, Difficulties, and Roots* (London: William Hunt, 1889).

The Mission

As a pastor, you are tasked with leading a church in accomplishing the mission Jesus gave to his people. The natural bent of the human heart is to become inwardly focused, which is anti-mission. Therefore, you must understand the Great Commission if you are to lead a church in accomplishing the mission.

- Tim Chester, *A Meal with Jesus: Discovering Grace, Community, and Mission around the Table* (Wheaton, IL: Crossway, 2011).
- Tim Chester and Steve Timmis, *Everyday Church: Gospel Communities on Mission* (Wheaton, IL: Crossway, 2013).
- Tim Chester and Steve Timmis, *Total Church: A Radical Reshaping around Gospel and Community* (Wheaton, IL: Crossway, 2008).
- Kevin DeYoung and Greg Gilbert, *What Is the Mission of the Church? Making Sense of Social Justice, Shalom, and the Great Commission* (Wheaton, IL: Crossway, 2011).
- Timothy Keller, *Center Church: Doing Balanced, Gospel-Centered Ministry in Your City* (Grand Rapids: Zondervan, 2012).
- Tony Merida, *Ordinary: How to Turn the World Upside Down* (Nashville: B&H, 2015).
- Tony Merida and Rick Morton, *Orphanology: Awakening to Gospel-Centered Adoption and Orphan Care* (Birmingham, AL: New Hope, 2011).
- John Piper, *Let the Nations Be Glad! The Supremacy of God in Missions*, 3rd ed. (Grand Rapids: Baker Academic, 2010).

Pastoral Ministry

Pastoral ministry is full of unique demands that are unlike any other area of leadership. Therefore, if we want to fight against the lies pastors tend to believe, we need to be adequately prepared for all the demands on a pastor's life.

- Richard Baxter, *The Reformed Pastor* (Carlisle, PA: Banner of Truth Trust, 1974).
- H. B. Charles Jr., *On Pastoring: A Short Guide to Living, Leading, and Ministering as a Pastor* (Chicago: Moody, 2016).
- Zach Eswine, *The Imperfect Pastor: Discovering Joy in Our Limitations through a Daily Apprenticeship with Jesus* (Wheaton, IL: Crossway, 2015).
- Jason Helopoulos, *The New Pastor's Handbook: Help and Encouragement for the First Years of Ministry* (Grand Rapids: Baker, 2015).
- John Piper, *Brothers, We Are Not Professionals: A Plea to Pastors for Radical Ministry,* updated and expanded edition (Nashville: B&H, 2013).
- Paul Tripp, *Dangerous Calling: Confronting the Unique Challenges of Pastoral Ministry* (Wheaton, IL: Crossway, 2012).
- Jared C. Wilson, *The Pastor's Justification: Applying the Work of Christ in Your Life and Ministry* (Wheaton, IL: Crossway, 2013).
- Timothy Z. Witmer, *The Shepherd Leader: Achieving Effective Shepherding in Your Church* (Phillipsburg, NJ: P&R, 2010).

Preaching

Preaching is much more than communicating in an engaging fashion for thirty to sixty minutes. A man who steps into a pulpit without a theology of preaching and an understanding of the aim of biblical preaching will do himself and his hearers great harm. Those aspiring to the office of teaching elder must grab hold of what it means to exposit the text of Scripture in a winsome and biblically faithful fashion. Never assume that you have grown beyond the need to refine your communication of Scripture.

- Bryan Chapell, *Christ-Centered Preaching: Redeeming the Expository Sermon*, 2nd ed. (Grand Rapids: Baker Academic, 2005).
- H. B. Charles Jr., *On Preaching: Personal & Pastoral Insights for the Preparation & Practice of Preaching* (Chicago: Moody, 2014).
- Timothy Keller, *Preaching: Communicating Faith in an Age of Skepticism* (New York: Viking, 2015).
- D. Martyn Lloyd-Jones, *Preaching and Preachers*, 40th anniversary ed. (Grand Rapids: Zondervan, 2012).
- Tony Merida, *The Christ-Centered Expositor: A Field Guide for Word-Driven Disciple Makers*, rev. ed. (Nashville: B&H Academic, 2016).
- John Piper, *The Supremacy of God in Preaching*, rev. ed. (Grand Rapids: Baker, 2004).
- J. C. Ryle, *Simplicity in Preaching* (Carlisle, PA: Banner of Truth, 2010).